MT. SHASTA

"The Shasta Coach" by William Keith, 1870

MT. SHASTA

HISTORY, LEGEND & LORE

by
MICHAEL ZANGER

CELESTIAL ARTS • BERKELEY, CALIFORNIA

Celestial Arts Publishing
Post Office Box 7327
Berkeley, California 94707
Printed in the United States of America.

Text and cover design by Ken Scott
Typesetting by Ann Flanagan Typography

Front cover, inside front and inside back cover
photographs of Mt. Shasta by Kevin Lahey

Library of Congress Cataloging-in-Publication Data

Zanger, Michael, 1941–
    Mt. Shasta / Michael Zanger.
        p.   cm.
    Includes bibliographical references.
    ISBN 0-89087-674-6
    1. Shasta, Mount (Calif.)—History.   I. Title.   II. Title: Mount
Shasta.
F868.S6Z34   1992
979.4′21—dc20   92-24720
                                                                       CIP

First printing 1992

1   2   3   4   5   /   96   95   94   93   92

Printed in Singapore

ACKNOWLEDGMENTS

I am indebted to the following people, whose help and enthusiasm for this project—which at times seemed as large as Mt. Shasta itself—made this book possible: librarian Dennis Freeman and his staff at the College of the Siskiyous Library for the use of their special collections and generous help in securing obscure documents and manuscripts; historian William Miesse for access to his private collections and endless help with historical details; historian and archaeologist Jeff LaLande for valuable information on Mt. Shasta's early explorers; Carleton Watkins biographer and photograph historian Peter Palmquist; archive photograph specialist Larry Vandemark; USGS historian Cliff Nelson; Peggy Appleman of the Smithsonian Institution for the loan of Wilkes Expedition material; Native American storyteller Tom Doty for information on Mt. Shasta's legends; California and Sierra Nevada historian Dr. David Beesley; logging and railroad historian Jerry Harmon; Forest Service archaeologist and anthropologist Julie Krieger; botanist Dr. William Bridge Cooke; Dorothy Park (Justin Sisson's great-granddaughter) for access to many of Sisson's personal papers; professional foresters James Nile, James DePree, David Marshall, Gordon Robinson, and Emmor Nile; logging historian Fred Gerding; Congressman John Seiberling; Congressional counsel Andy Wiessner; lumberers Mario Marchi and Howard Peterson; Siskiyou County librarians Terry Thompson, Marilee Jordan, and Kathy Fueston; William Jones of the Meriam Library at California State University, Chico; Richard Ogar of The Bancroft Library; Lee Apperson of the Sisson Hatchery Museum; The Siskiyou County Museum and Historical Society; The Mazamas; The Klamath County Museum; The Oregon Historical Society; and Sierra, Jenny, and Chris for their unlimited patience and support.

Thanks also to: Michelle Berditchevsky, Nancy Blair, Steve Bollock, Anita Butler, Robert Casbeer, Paul Dawson, Jane English, Gene Fleet, Marilyn Ford, Leroy Foster, Steve Gerace, Leonardo Gonzales, Michael Hendryx, Phil Holecek, Steve Johnson, Larry Jordan, Libby Knight, Kevin Lahey, Eleanor Mauro, Linda Ragsdale, Jim Ray, Phil Rhodes, Cheryl Yambrach Rose, Bee Rowe, Chris Schneider, Perry Sims, Kate Spelman, John Swanson, Robert Webb, Leila Whitcombe, Ernest Woodfield, and Lynda Zehsazian.

And, lastly, special thanks to Ed and Rosie Stuhl for all the times in front of the fireplace with tea, good conversation, and laughter.

—Michael Zanger
1992

TABLE *of* CONTENTS

Mt. Shasta and its secondary peak, Shastina, from the North KEVIN LAHEY PHOTOGRAPH

INTRODUCTION

Mt. Shasta stands in solitary dominance as the most striking mountain in Northern California. Its power exerts itself first on the eyes. To see the mountain from a distance is to experience a transformative awareness of something larger and more beautiful than its mere physical presence. Mt. Shasta, virtually unknown by Anglo's until a century and a half ago, is not only visually stunning, but also carries a rich history of exploration and legend, mythical and spiritual odyssey, and contemporary environmental debate.

The view from the summit of Mt. Shasta evokes a feeling of timelessness. To the east, the pastel ridges of Medicine Lake Highlands stretch to Nevada. To the north, Cascade peaks Mt. McLoughlin, Mt. Thielsen, and Mt. Mazama (Crater Lake) rise above the clouds. To the south, the cleft of the Sacramento River Canyon gently winds, then broadens in the Central Valley. To the west rise the jumble of the Klamath Mountains and Castle Crags. Scattered over Shasta Valley north of the mountain are small knolls of lava—products of minor eruptions that broke through the landscape many thousands of years ago.

This volcanic landscape and Shasta's steaming summit fumaroles are a reminder of Shasta's fiery origin. Were it not for the snaking of an interstate highway to remind one of the twentieth century, the whole scene could be prehistoric, as if viewed through a time-warp.

Mt. Shasta has one of the largest base-to-summit rises of the world's mountains—over 11,000 feet—and with a volume of more than 80 cubic miles, is the largest volcanic peak in the continental United States. Indeed, if Shastina, Mt. Shasta's secondary cone, stood alone, it would be the third highest mountain in the Cascade range. Shasta is home to California's largest glaciers and a diverse wealth of animal and plant life. The mountain's main cone has a symmetrical shape unbroken by extensive erosion, which indicates that in geologic time Shasta is a relative youngster. And there is plenty of evidence that it has erupted frequently during the past ten thousand years: The lower slopes contain broad ridges of pyroclastic material (ejected rock fragments) and mud and lava flows extending as far as 20 miles from the mountain. The upper slopes consist of pumice, ash, and jagged, eroded rock ridges that are remnants of the mountain when it was younger.

The world's great singular mountains like Kilimanjaro, Fuji, Kailas, and Shasta have been lodestones for history. Explorers, naturalists, poets, and saints have been drawn to these giants, and from them has resulted a wellspring of scientific study, art, legends, and lore.

·9·

Mt. Shasta from Strawberry Valley KEVIN LAHEY PHOTOGRAPH

PREFACE

ere is a remarkable story of a mountain and the culture that formed around it. Shasta rose from confusion as to name, place, and height. It is a peak that was climbed from early on and often, sometimes by long-skirted high-spirited women climbers from the local ranches. It soon attracted an amazing array of eminent, talented, tireless, charming fanatics. They came to it for spiritual, ecological, magical, athletic, economic and artistic reasons. Meanwhile around the base relentless timber companies took out a staggering quantity of top-quality ponderosa pine. Wilderness protection (37,000 acres) came none too soon. It is a beacon for all of northern California, at the headwaters of rivers that flow out through the Golden Gate. I did my own windy climb on it at sixteen. Mt. Shasta is a mountain with a different facet, a different magic, for each angle of view. This excellent book fills a long-felt need. Michael Zanger has given us a little gem of mountain appreciation and information.

Gary Snyder
Pulitzer Prize-winning poet

Mt. Shasta KEVIN LAHEY PHOTOGRAPH

· 12 ·

"Mount Shasta" by Frederick A. Butman, 1857

CHAPTER 1

THE QUESTION *of* DISCOVERY

MOUNT SHASTA WAS THE LAST MAJOR MOUNTAIN OF THE PACIFIC NORTHWEST TO BE DISCOVERED BY EURO-AMERICAN EXPLORERS. Rainier, Hood, St. Helens, Baker, and St. Elias were all named and mapped before 1800. The reason Mt. Shasta remained unknown for so long is evident by looking at a map of the western states: it lay inland far enough from the coast to be unseen by sailing ships and was located approximately midway between the British settlements at Fort Vancouver at the mouth of the Columbia River and the Spanish enclaves in Monterey and San Francisco. Shasta was not seen by explorers until they had journeyed overland nearly 300 miles from these settlements into unknown territory.

While historians are in agreement as to *why* Mt. Shasta was discovered so late, they are in disagreement as to *when* and *by whom* the mountain was first sighted.

LA PÉROUSE

During the summer of 1786 the French sea captain Jean-François de Galoup, Comte de La Pérouse (also known as Jean de La Pérouse), completing an exploration of the Pacific, sailed south along the present Oregon and California coasts bound for the Spanish settlements at Monterey. La Pérouse made the following entry in his ship's log for September 5 and 6, 1786:

> Our latitude was 42°58′56″; and our longitude by our timekeepers 127°5′20″. At two o'clock we were about a league distant from Cape Blanco, which bore north-east by east. I con-

tinued to run along the land, standing to the south-south-east. At the distance of three or four leagues, we perceived only the summits of the mountains above the clouds. They were covered with trees, and we could see no snow. . . . Uncertain of the direction of the coast, which had never been explored, I kept under an easy sail to the south-south-west. At day-break we still saw the land, which stretched from the north to north by east. I steered south-east by east to get near it; but at seven in the morning a thick mist occasioned us to lose sight of it.

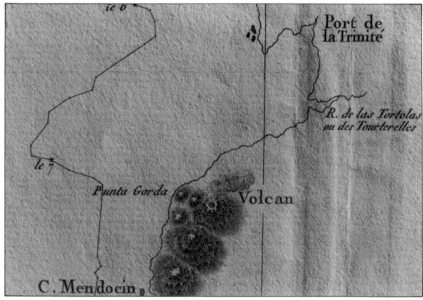

A portion of Jean de La Pérouse's map showing his 1786 voyage down the

North American west coast, and the mysterious "volcan" north of

California's Cape Mendocino he sighted from the sea on September 7th.

The following day's logs continued to record the southward voyage, but also contained a surprising observation:

We found the weather in this part of America less clear than in higher latitudes, where the navigators enjoyed, at least by intervals, the sight of everything that was above their horizon; for to us the land never once appeared distinct in all its parts. On the 7th the mist was still thicker than the day before. It cleared up, however, towards noon, and we saw the tops of mountains to the east, at a considerable distance. As we had made a southern course, it is evident, that from the latitude of 42° the coast begins to run to the east. Our latitude observed at noon was 40°48′30″ north; our longitude by our timekeepers 126°59′45″ west. I continued to steer so as to get nearer the land, from which I was only four leagues distant at the approach of night. We then perceived a volcano on the summit of the mountain which bore east from us. The flame was very vivid; but a thick fog soon concealed it from our sight. Deeming it prudent again to increase our distance from the land, as I was apprehensive, that, by following a course parallel to the coast, I might fall in with some rock or island at a little distance from the continent, I stood towards the offing again.

The next day the weather worsened with fog and clouds that prevented any sight of land. After sighting the flaming mountain, La Pérouse's two frigates continued sailing south through foul weather for the next seven days, reaching Monterey on September 15, where the Mexican governor was awaiting their arrival. No mention of the mysterious volcano appeared in the ship's log again. La Pérouse's maps and journals were eventually sent to Paris where they were prepared for publication in 1797. It is

Jean de La Pérouse

COURTESY EDWARD STUHL COLLECTION

important to note that the volcano in question appearing on the published map is located *on the coast,* but how faithfully the original maps were reproduced is unknown. La Pérouse was never able to explain in greater detail the volcano he saw, for the famous navigator, his ships, and his crew all disappeared in the South Pacific in 1788.

A look at a modern map of the west coasts of Oregon and California reveals that La Pérouse's navigation was remarkably accurate. His reckoning of latitude off Cape Blanco on September 5, 1786, was within 20 miles of the true position of this coastal headland north of Port Orford, Oregon. We may assume, then, that La Pérouse's observed position on September 7 was also reasonably accurate. His recorded latitude and longitude for this date place him near the coast at Eureka, California—nearly equidistant from Mt. Shasta and Mt. Lassen. Although neither mountain can be seen from the sea, both are within range to view the smoke and flames of a major volcanic eruption.

However, the scant information in La Pérouse's log gives us no more clue of what he may have seen: An eruption of Mt. Shasta or Mt. Lassen? A forest fire atop one of the coastal peaks? Euro-American records of the inland regions were, of course, very sparse during the late 1700s and very early 1800s, made primarily by the Spanish missionaries well south of Mt. Shasta and the fur trappers near the Columbia River well to the north. No hint of any Cascade volcanic eruption appears in the journals and records of these frontier outposts to substantiate La Pérouses's logs. The Native American tribes living near Mt. Shasta told legends describing smoke and fire-belching mountains, but the myth / reality distinctions and dates are so vague that they are of little use in accurately pinpointing historical events.

·15·

DON LUIS ARGUELLO

The early Spaniards in Alta California, the former Spanish and Mexican province that today comprises the state of California, were not greatly concerned with exploration. They usually sent out expeditions to search for favorable sites for new missions or to assess the probability of foreign intrusion. Spanish expedition leaders kept diaries and journals, but the distances, landmarks, and attention to geographical details in them are inconsistent. Except for mention of major rivers and mountains, and occasionally settlements, the Spanish explorers' routes are difficult to trace from their journal entries.

One of the first inland expeditions—and one from which diaries have survived—was led by Don Luis Arguello in May 1817. Arguello, who later became governor of California, was accompanied by a priest, Fray Narciso Duran, who recorded the progress of the exploratory trip in his personal journal. The party left the Presidio at San Francisco in two small boats on May 13, and proceeded to sail northeast up the Sacramento River. It is unclear from Fray Duran's journals how far up the river the expedition eventually reached, but before they turned around on May 20, 1817, Fray Duran made the following journal entry:

> At about ten leagues to the northwest of this place we saw the very high hill called by soldiers that went near its slope Jesus Maria. It is entirely covered with snow. They say that a great river of the same name runs near it, and that it enters the Sacramento River, and they conjecture that it may be some branch of the Columbia. This I have heard from some soldier; let the truth be what it may. To-day we went four leagues up the river toward the north and northwest.

(The reference to the "Columbia" can be confusing. The Spaniards used the term generically in reference to the north-ernmost area of interior California, of which they had only a vague notion.)

During the 1920s two noted scholars offered theories on Arguello's expedition. Ansel Hall, chief naturalist for the National Park Service, concluded that the Spaniards on that expedition were the first white people to see Mt. Shasta. Francis Farquhar, a historian of California and the Sierra Nevada, theorized that Arguello's party journeyed no farther than the junction of the Feather and Sacramento rivers, a little north of the present city of Sacramento. With no more evidence than Fray Duran's sparse journal entries, we can only guess as to the party's northernmost point during the 1817 journey, and what great snow-covered mountain they saw.

Arguello's expedition took place during May, a time when the Sacramento and its tributary rivers were high and full with water from spring thaw in the mountains. Fray Duran concluded it would be easier to follow the river on land during the autumn dry season, perhaps as far as the mysterious Sierra Nevada. His May 20, 1817, journal entry reads;

> The course of the river from here on could be followed better by land than by water, and the vast Sierra Nevada be examined, which lands, it is likely, may be settled by innumerable natives. Once the pass in the Sierra is discovered, which the said end seems to offer, we would be able to ascertain the truth of what the Indians have told us for some years past, that on the other side of the Sierra Nevada there are people like our soldiers. We have never been able to clear up the matter and know whether they are Spanish from New Mexico, or English from the Columbia, or Russians from La Bodega.

THE RUSSIANS

The Russian explorers who settled in the Bodega Bay area in the early nineteenth century may have been significant in the discovery of Mt. Shasta. Fort Ross, 20 miles north of Bodega Bay, was founded by the Russians in 1812. They sent a number of expeditions and trapping brigades up the small coastal rivers, but none went as far as the Sacramento drainage.

In 1841 a member of the Russian fur-trapping colony at Fort Ross climbed Mt. Saint Helena and named it in honor of Empress Helena of Russia, placing a plaque to mark the occasion. Mt. Saint Helena, at 4,344 feet, is one of the highest coastal peaks and is only 40 miles inland from Fort Ross. Mt. Shasta, Mt. Lassen, and some of the peaks of the northern Sierra Nevada are visible from its summit, but we can only surmise that the Russians who climbed Mt. Saint Helena before 1841 saw Mt. Shasta—historical records tell us little. However, an intriguing clue exists that still plays an important role in the search for the source of the name "Shasta": The Russian word for "white," or "pure," is *tchastal*. Perhaps notes, journals, or diaries from the early Russian explorers, still preserved within the archives of what is now the Commonwealth of Independent States, will some day emerge from dust and oblivion to shed more light on the enigma of Mt. Shasta's name and discovery.

ARGUELLO'S SECOND EXPEDITION

Don Luis Arguello was sent out again in the fall of 1821 to investigate a rumor that a group of English or Americans had entered California north of San Francisco. The Arguello party left San Francisco on October 18, 1821, accompanied this time by Fray Blas Ordaz, who kept the journals. Journeying up the Sacramento River again, they reached their northernmost point on October 30. On that day, Fray Ordaz made the following entry in his diary:

> The place where we are is situated at the foot of the Sierra Madre, whence there have been indistinctly seen by the English interpreter, Juan Antonio, two mountains called Los Quates—the Twins—on opposite side of which are the presidio and the Columbia River.

Arguello's expedition then turned west, passed down the eastern slope of the Coast Range, and reached San Rafael on November 12, 1821.

Again, the Arguello expedition journals are unclear as to the distances traveled. However, Fray Ordaz did record the names and descriptions of several large Native American villages that the expedition passed en route. From this information, anthropologist and ethnologist Dr. Alfred Kroeber estimated that Arguello's second expedition went as far north as the present city of Chico, California.

Historians agree that two possibilities exist in reference to Fray Ordaz's "Twins": The party may have seen Mt. Shasta and Mt. Lassen—Shasta's greater distance would have tended to reduce the nearly 4,000-foot elevation discrepancy between the two, making them appear nearly equal. Another, more likely, explanation is that the party saw Mt. Lassen and its adjacent promontory, Broke-off Mountain. In fact, John C. Fremont, encamped below Red Bluff in the spring of 1846, referred to these two peaks as "The Sisters."

Arguello left us with tantalizing but inconclusive evidence that he was the first white explorer to see Mt. Shasta. And the mystery remains, for it still cannot be said with assurance that any of these intrepid, early explorers actually saw the mountain.

"Shasta Butte" by John J. Young, 1855. Done for the Williamson-Abbot Railroad Survey

CHAPTER 2

TRAPPERS, EXPLORERS, & THE NAME "SHASTA"

FROM MT. SHASTA'S SUMMIT, CLIMBERS CAN SEE TWO DISTINCT NORTH-SOUTH CORRIDORS THAT PASS ON OPPOSITE SIDES OF THE MOUNTAIN. The first route comes south from Klamath Falls and Klamath Lake near the California-Oregon border, crosses a broad valley north of the rugged Medicine Lake Highland, then passes between Whaleback Mountain and the eastern flanks of Mt. Shasta. The route then curves southeast toward the Fall River and Pit River drainages and continues south to the Sacramento Valley. This is the likely route for a traveler on the east side of the Cascade Range.

The second track, for the wayfarer who passes along the western flank of the Cascades, crosses the east-west running Siskiyou Mountains, passes south through Shasta Valley before reaching the Sacramento River headwaters on Shasta's west side, then follows the steep river canyon to the wide Sacramento Valley. These corridors, widely separated by Mt. Shasta's huge presence, were probably found and used by Native Americans for centuries before being discovered by the foreign explorers and fur trappers of the early nineteenth century.

HUDSON'S BAY COMPANY

Twenty years before the California Gold Rush, Hudson's Bay Company fur trappers opened a route southward from the Columbia River in the Pacific Northwest, over the Siskiyou Mountains, to California. The route evolved into a wagon road for settlers during the 1840s and 1850s, and by the 1880s became the roadbed for the railroad that now links California and the Pacific Northwest. Interstate 5, a major U.S. highway, closely parallels the route the original explorers took and offers today's travelers a view of Mt. Shasta for nearly 200 miles.

Many of the original fur traders and explorers of the Pacific Northwest worked for the Hudson's Bay Company. The company was granted a Royal Charter in 1670 by the King of England for nearly 1.5 million square miles of Hudson Bay watershed—almost 40 percent of Canada—which included all land not occupied by the Russians or the French. The "Honourable Company," as it was first called, eventually became the Hudson's Bay Company and by the early 1820s had a profitable operation established at Fort Vancouver at the mouth of the Columbia River.

The beaver was as important commercially to the Pacific Northwest as the bison was to the Great Plains, and large fur-trapping parties were sent out annually. For decades company expeditions explored and trapped extensively in northern and central Oregon, far out of sight of Mt. Shasta, but in the early 1820s conflicts with Native Americans on the Willamette River caused the company to begin sending scout parties farther south toward California.

The history of the fur trade, as colorful and adventurous as it was, does not enjoy quite the level of literary and historical notoriety as the Gold Rush, the classic drama of the West. Many famous and legendary characters explored and trapped during the heyday of the Pacific Northwest fur trade, but the early fur trappers—the "Sinbads of the wilderness," as author Washington Irving called them—did not keep clear records or journals. Their diaries were often scrawled on coarse paper or beaver skins with pencil, or even charcoal, and often as not looked like hieroglyphics to fur company agents, and later historians, who tried to decipher the accounts. In addition, the Hudson's Bay Company, by far the largest and most important of all the fur-trapping enterprises, kept its trappers' journals, records, and maps under lock and key as company secrets; it did not want competitors to know where the rich trapping grounds were located. Hence, a truly complete and accurate history of this important time in the West is not easily compiled. There are several gaps, especially regarding Mt. Shasta.

PETER SKENE OGDEN

Hudson's Bay Company trapper Peter Skene Ogden left Fort Vancouver on September 12, 1826, and followed the Columbia River east as far as The Dalles, where he met additional company employees. The group turned south, crossed central Oregon, and arrived at Klamath Marsh, east of Crater Lake, on December 12.

It is significant to note that Ogden's original diary of this trip, the 1826–1827 "Snake Country Journal," languished for decades in the Hudson's Bay Company's London archives. In 1905 Agnes Laut transcribed Ogden's journals, then published them in 1910 in the *Oregon Historical Quarterly*. This transcription was the basis of historical reference until 1961, when the Hudson's Bay Record Society published another version of the journal with the addition of an editor's interpretations.

On December 12, 1826, Ogden recorded his course as south. No other course information is again given until January 29, 1827. Ogden's December 25 journal entry, from an area fitting the description of Tule Lake, northeast of Mt. Shasta, reads:

On both sides of us the mountains are very high . . . one in particular high above all others pointed and well covered with snow—and from its height must be at a considerable distance from us. Our Guides inform'd us beyond these Mountains reside the Sastise a nation they are at present at war with.

Although Ogden mentioned the Sastise, he did not assign a name to the high mountain, nor did he mention it again in later journal entries. On February 10, 1827, he wrote:

> Here we are among the Sastise. Course this day west. The stream we are on has no connection with the Clammitte [Klamath] River; it flows south then west to a large river. These Indians know nothing of the ocean.

Peter Skene Ogden in 1824.

COURTESY LIBRARY OF CONGRESS

Then on February 14, while traveling northwest through the Rogue River Valley, Ogden made his now-famous journal entry:

> I have named this river Sastise River. There is a mountain equal in height to Mount Hood or Vancouver, I have named Mt. Sastise. I have given these names from the tribes of Indians.

In April and May 1827 Ogden retraced his route back through Northern California to the headwaters of the Pit River, which he named for the numerous elk-trapping pits Native Americans had dug in the area. Ogden then turned northeast to the Snake River and Fort Nez Perce.

John Arrowsmith's 1834 map of British North America, based on Peter Skene Ogden's sketch maps, was the first map to use the name "Mt. Shasty" for any mountain. This was the first map to show that today's Mt. McLoughlin in Oregon was actually the first mountain to be named "Mt. Shasty." Note the large unnamed mountain where today's Mt. Shasta is located.

COURTESY WILLIAM MIESSE COLLECTION

With the publication of the Agnes Laut transcription of Ogdens' journals, more than eighty years after his expedition, Ogden found favor with historians and was recognized as the discoverer and namer of Mt. Shasta. But in 1926 naturalist and ethnologist Dr. C. Hart Merriam offered a challenge. Merriam, studying the source of the name "Shasta," noticed some interesting differences among the names of the Native American tribes in southern Oregon and Northern California: "Shasta," a tribe northwest of the mountain, had *not* been the name of the Shasta tribe members for themselves, but the name the Klamath tribe used in referring to them. Merriam thought that Ogden therefore got the name "Sastise" from the Klamath tribe and applied the name to the Rogue River and Mt. McLoughlin when he entered the Klamath's territory. Merriam also found that the first maps of the area showed a "Shasty" or "Shaste" river *northwest* of the "Clamet River," and the named peak well *north* of the 42nd parallel—the California-Oregon border—and the Klamath River.

Merriam's theory received little publicity, and for years the question of which mountain and river Peter Ogden actually saw and named remained only an academic question among historians. That is, until U.S. Forest Service archaeologist Jeff LaLande began unravelling the puzzle in the early 1980s. LaLande found that the Laut translation of Ogden's journal had been abridged and paraphrased considerably from the original, and that the 1961 Hudson's Bay Record Society version had taken interpretational liberties in key areas. It was left for LaLande to retrace Ogden's route using the original journal records.

After his journey, LaLande concluded that Ogden had clearly followed southern Oregon's Rogue River and viewed Mt. McLoughlin, naming *it* "Mt. Sastise." LaLande also speculated that the mysterious unnamed mountain Ogden saw on December 26, 1826, from near Tule Lake must have been Mt. Shasta. Ogden's journal maps have never been found, leaving a void in the history of his 1826–1827 journey. Nevertheless, history has effectively granted Peter Ogden the title of first Euro-American

discoverer of Mt. Shasta. Although this may be true in reference to his observed mountain "high above all others," the mountain that Ogden named Mt. Sastise, or Shasta, is almost certainly today's Mt. McLoughlin.

HUDSON'S BAY COMPANY TRAPPERS

The next person in the chain of explorers to visit the Mt. Shasta area was Jedediah Smith, senior partner in the Rocky Mountain Fur Company, and famous as the first American to journey overland to California. Ordered to leave California by Mexican authorities in 1828, Smith made his way up the Sacramento Valley to Cottonwood Creek, near today's Red Bluff, then northwest through the Trinity Mountains to the coast. His group was ambushed by Native Americans at the mouth of the Umpqua River, and all but Smith and three others were killed.

Losing all their traps and furs, the survivors escaped to Fort Vancouver where they related their story to Dr. John McLoughlin, chief factor for the Hudson's Bay Company in the Pacific Northwest. Smith offered McLoughlin a deal: He would guide a Hudson's Bay Company party to the rich trapping grounds he had just left if they would help him recover his lost goods. The offer was accepted, and McLoughlin sent out Alexander McLeod, who succeeded in recovering Smith's furs and belongings and sending them back to Fort Vancouver before continuing down into the Sacramento Valley to trap. Smith's maps were lost, but his diary was recovered. It contains entries indicating a "Rogers Peak" seen and named when the party turned west to the Pacific Coast. (Harrison Rogers was Smith's secretary and clerk during the trip.) A few years later, certain maps of the area showed "Rogers Peak" for Mt. Lassen and "Simpson Peak" for Mt. Shasta. (George Simpson, governor of the entire North American Hudson's Bay Company territory, visited the Pacific Northwest in 1828.) Some historians think it was Jedediah Smith who named Mt. Shasta "Mt. Simpson" in

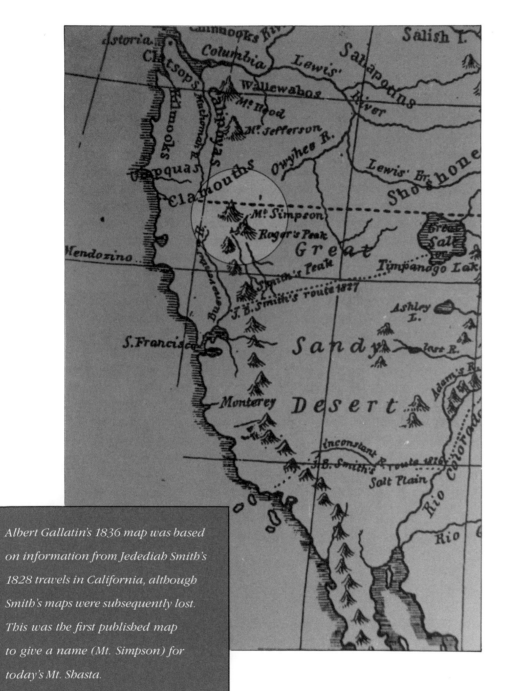

Albert Gallatin's 1836 map was based on information from Jedediah Smith's 1828 travels in California, although Smith's maps were subsequently lost. This was the first published map to give a name (Mt. Simpson) for today's Mt. Shasta.

honor of the governor, sometime after the two met in 1828. Smith's maps were never found, and he was later killed by Native Americans before he could offer more details on his trip up the Sacramento Valley.

The Hudson's Bay Company gave Alexander McLeod travel information taken from Peter Skene Ogden's reports, including the location of "Sastise Mountain." During McLeod's return journey to Fort Vancouver in the late autumn and winter of 1829, he and his group were caught in a severe snowstorm near what McLeod called "Chaste Mount," on a tributary of the upper Sacramento River. They were forced to cache their furs and goods, reaching Fort Vancouver empty-handed after considerable hardship. What mountain McLeod meant when he referred to "Chaste Mount" is not completely clear.

It is not uncommon for bad weather to obscure the sight of Mt. Shasta and the other Cascade peaks for weeks at a time during the winter months; it's possible that McLeod never saw Ogden's original "Sastise Mountain" (present-day Mt. McLoughlin) when he journeyed south at the beginning of his trapping expedition. It is likely, however, that McLeod was the first person to transfer the name from this mountain, albeit unknowingly, to today's Mt. Shasta. (Some historians have cited the name of the McCloud River east of the mountain—in spite of the spelling difference—as proof that McLeod's party was encamped nearby. However, the name may just as likely have come from Ross McCloud, a prominent settler who came to the area nearly twenty-five years later.)

Hudson's Bay Company trappers were more interested in pelts and furs than keeping track of geographic names. Ten years after McLeod's trip, George Simpson, who was head of the Hudson's Bay Company during McLeod's tenure, referred to the very large mountain near the site of the McLeod party's disaster as "Pit Mountain," so-called for the large pitfalls dug by Native Americans along a nearby river to catch game. (It has never been clear if the location was the same as "Pit River," where

·23·

Washington Hood's 1838 "United States Territory of Oregon" map placed "Mt. Shasty" at the location of today's Mt. McLoughlin and "Pit Mountain" at today's Mt. Shasta. Note the "Shasty" and "Nasty" Rivers as tributaries of the "Rouge Clamet" and located in the Oregon Territory.

COURTESY WILLIAM MIESSE COLLECTION

·24·

Peter Skene Ogden had also discovered animal trapping pits.) Simpson wrote of the area:

> In fact, this mountain was notorious as the worst part of their journey: for about ten years before, our trappers, being overtaken by a violent storm, had lost, on this very ground, the whole of their furs, and nearly three hundred horses.

After McLeod's 1829 expedition, the route from the Columbia River to California's Central Valley was used by increasing numbers of trappers and explorers. Each successive party had more information, more detailed descriptions, and maps of the fur-trapping grounds that had been brought back to Hudson's Bay Company's McLoughlin by previous trapping parties. Although the maps of the area became increasingly more accurate and detailed, they typically reflected the fact that the cartographers had to work from incomplete or secondhand information. During the two decades following Ogden's 1826–1827 expedition through Northern California, Mt. Shasta appeared on different maps with the following names: Pit Mountain, Mt. Simpson, Mt. Jackson, Snowy Butte, Sasty Peak, and Mt. Tsashtl.

THE CONFUSION OF NAMES

One of the first nontrappers to visit the area surrounding Mt. Shasta was Hall Jackson Kelley, a patriotic Boston schoolmaster who entertained grand visions of colonizing Oregon. Traveling north from California in 1834 with American trapper Ewing Young, Kelley passed within sight of many of the Cascade peaks, taking it upon himself to call them "The Presidents' Range." Kelley's maps, handdrawn with his own reckonings of latitude and longitude, were filed with the Department of State in 1839 showing Mt. Shasta as "Mt. Jackson." Kelley, and his claims to the U.S. Government for compensation for "settling the Oregon

Territory," were never taken seriously. Surprisingly, however, "Mt. Jackson" appeared on some maps as late as 1845, finding favor with an American public still sympathetic with former President Andrew Jackson's pro-expansion philosophy.

In 1841 an overland contingent of Navy Lieutenant Charles Wilkes's round-the-world United States Exploring Expedition traveled from the Columbia River southward through the Sacramento Valley. Henry Eld, the expedition cartographer, knew the location of "Shaste Mountain" (present-day Mt. McLoughlin) in Oregon Territory from previous maps and information obtained from the Hudson's Bay Company. Yet, for unknown reasons, Eld transposed the name to the present Mt. Shasta.

When Wilkes's maps were published in 1844 it was the first time that "Mt. Shaste," by any spelling, appeared on a map clearly identifying *today's* Mt. Shasta. Thus, the mountain—and its transposed name—became official on U.S. maps. (Later, General John C. Fremont added to the name-change drama by shifting one of Shasta's old names, "Pit Mountain," to today's Mt. McLoughlin on his 1848 maps.)

A brief description of Mt. Shasta in the 1846 *The Oregon Territory* reflected the degree of confusion surrounding the mountain's name—and height—at that time:

> Pitt Mountain, or, as it is called by the Americans, Mount Jackson, or as by the trappers, Mount Shaste, is said to be 20,000 feet above the level of the sea.

By the 1850s settlers began moving into Shasta Valley and the surrounding area, and cattle were being driven from central California over the Siskiyou Mountains into Oregon. Yreka, Weaverville, and other camps became overnight boomtowns as the Gold Rush displaced the fur trade. Many American trappers that passed through California began to settle there as the fur trade diminished. To most easterners, California was still considered the wild west. Stephen Meek had trapped for the Hudson's Bay Company

Hall Jackson Kelley's 1839 map showed today's Mt. Shasta as "Mt. Jackson," and today's Sacramento River as "Kelley's R."

Hall Jackson Kelley

·25·

and finally settled in the Scott Valley west of Mt. Shasta. One spring, Meek returned to Lexington, Missouri, to visit his brother and sister. While relating some of the many incidents of his mountain life to family and friends, he was asked by a young lady, "Mr. Meek, didn't you never get killed by none of them Indians and bears?" "Oh, yes, madam," Meek replied gravely, "I was frequently killed!"

Settlers and miners now journeyed regularly to Northern California through the Sacramento River canyon or along the Pit River. Military Pass Road, traversing Mt. Shasta's eastern flank, became the standard route from Ft. Crook near Fall River to Yreka and Ft. Jones. This scenic dirt road still exists, closely following the original wagon track as it connects California highways 89 and 97.

In a scant two decades after Peter Ogden and the Hudson's Bay Company fur trappers entered unknown territory, the hills and valleys surrounding Mt. Shasta changed from wilderness to Gold Rush-inspired civilization. Mt. Shasta was now a familiar landmark and would soon become a focal point for climbers, scientists, artists, railroad surveyors, and entrepreneurs.

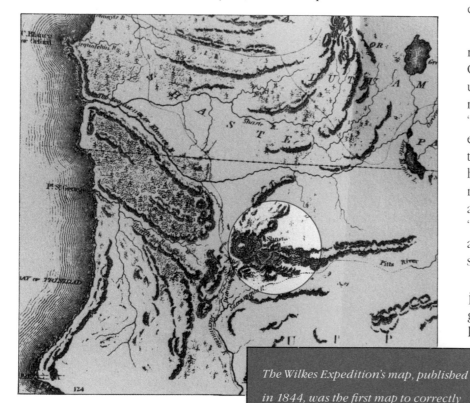

The Wilkes Expedition's map, published in 1844, was the first map to correctly name, by any spelling variant, today's Mt. Shasta.

THE NAME "SHASTA"

The source of the name "Shasta" has caused controversy among historians, anthropologists, and linguists for years. Near the beginning of the twentieth century Alfred Kroeber, an authority on Native Americans in California, stated that its origin was veiled in doubt and obscurity and would never be established. Indeed, if historians agree on anything, it is that the name derives from several different sources, all crossing history's timeline at different points to find places in anthropological and ethnographic studies, on maps, and in history books. Errors committed to print are difficult to correct, and it is often equally difficult to find out why and how they originated.

In writings and references through the years Shasta is referred to variously as Shastasla, Sasta, Sasty, Sastise, Shasty, Chaste, Chestet, Chasty, Shastl, and Tschastl. The earliest known use of the name "Shasta" (not referring to the mountain) was made in 1814 by trapper Alexander Henry when discussing the "Shastasla" tribe in Oregon's Willamette Valley, which is considerably north of Mt. Shasta. The relationship, if any, of Mt. Shasta to this tribe or to any of the surrounding Native American tribes has never been determined. But "Shasta" was definitely not the name given to the mountain by any of the tribes. The Klamath and Modoc tribes called it "Melaikshi." The Yana's term was "Wahkalu." The Wintun called it "Bohem Puyok" (Great Peak), and the Achomawi and Atsugewi referred to the giant mountain simply as "Yet."

Prior to the publication of Peter Skene Ogden's 1826–1827 journal in 1910, there had been much speculation as to the origin and meaning of the word "Shasta." In 1841 Horatio Hale, a linguist with the Wilkes Expedition, observed:

The Lutuami or Clamet Indians seem to be engaged in constant hostilities with their neighbors, the Saste and Palaik. These two tribes live, the former to the southwest, and the latter to the southeast of the Lutuami.

Scholfield's 1851 Gold Region map correctly placed and spelled "Mt. Shasta" for the first time.

In 1907 ethnologist Roland B. Dixon concluded that "Shasta" referred to a prominent Native American living in Shasta Valley in the 1850s named Shastika. Dixon probably fell victim to a dilemma that continually plagues anthropologists: by the time he began his studies, the Native Americans in question had already been scattered, and, in many ways, their cultures had disintegrated from the catastrophic effect of encroaching white settlement. Therefore, the territories, place names, and languages of the indigenous Native Americans were no longer exact, a condition that was undoubtedly responsible for the many claimed origins of the "Shasta" name.

The first publication and subsequent interpretations of Ogden's 1826–1827 journal provided strong evidence that the Klamath tribe referred to their southern neighbors as the *Sastise.* This seems to be the name that finally evolved, with cultural, linguistic, academic, and cartographic help into today's "Shasta."

Maps, as they change over the years, reflect the history of both geographical knowledge and place names. The earliest appearance of the name "Shasta" (in variant form) in print was on John Arrowsmith's "Map of British North America," published in 1834 for the Hudson's Bay Company. Arrowsmith's 1834 map was correct, based on Ogden's information, in applying the name to a peak north of the California-Oregon border but it was not the peak we know as Mt. Shasta. The significant error by the Wilkes expedition in transferring names was made many years later.

We know now that the actual mountain named by Peter Skene Ogden was almost certainly today's Mt. McLoughlin. Ogden was the first white explorer to bestow the name "Shasta" on any mountain, but it is unlikely he intended the name for the mountain now known by it. By the time of the Gold Rush, the litany of Native American names, French-Canadian pronunciations, Presidential recognition, and grammatical aberrations had nearly run its course. "Mt. Shasta" appeared on N. Scholfield's 1851 "Gold Region" map correctly spelled, located, and accepted.

In 1890, Albert Gatschet's Klamath language dictionary stated that the Klamath tribe, adjoining the "Shaste" tribe on the north and east, used the name "Shasti" or "Sasti" for their neighbors. Also in 1890, California historian Hubert Bancroft claimed that the name was a derivation of the French word *chaste,* for "pure" or "white," applied by early French-Canadian trappers. And still other historians subscribed to the theory that "Shasta" derived from the Russian *Tchastal,* also meaning "pure" or "white," on the assumption Mt. Shasta had been seen and named by Russian colonists at Fort Ross.

Castle Lake and Mt Shasta

Casting down Mt Shasta

The Thumb Lower Slope of Mt Shasta

Summit of Mt Shasta

Illustration from an 1887 Harper's Weekly *travel article on Mt. Shasta and the surrounding area.* "The ascent of the mountain is not dangerous or difficult, except as taxing to their utmost the powers of endurance and the soundness of heart and lungs."

·28·

CHAPTER 3

THE FIRST CLIMBS

W HEN GENERAL JOHN C. FREMONT TRAVELED PAST THE EASTERN SIDE OF MT. SHASTA ON HIS WAY TO KLAMATH LAKE IN 1846, HE NOTED THAT THE MOUNTAIN APPEARED TO BE "NEARLY THE HEIGHT OF MONT BLANC." Two years earlier Fremont wrote of the Cascade peaks in general, "They have never yet known the tread of human foot; sternly drawn against the sky, they look so high, so steep, so snowy and rocky, that it appears almost impossible to climb them." Major roles in the Mexican War and the struggle for California statehood prevented Fremont, known as the "Pathfinder," from returning to Mt. Shasta, but rumors persisted that he had been thwarted three times in attempting to climb the mountain. Never one to admit defeat, he chose not to mention the climbs, if, in fact, they had ever been attempted.

General John C. Fremont. Daguerreotype by the famous Civil War photographer, Mathew Brady. The tiny print at the bottom is of Mt. Shasta.

COURTESY LIBRARY OF CONGRESS

·29·

"Forest Camp Shastl Peak" Unknown artist, from the Fremont expedition of 1845–46.
First published in Fremont's memoirs in 1887

Climbing mountains was not an especially popular pastime for early miners and settlers in the West unless there was a tangible reward, such as gold, for their efforts. Yet, Shasta must have exerted a strong attraction to the people in its surrounding area; from 1854 to 1856 no less than forty people (five women and thirty-five men) ascended the mountain.

The first was Elias Davidson Pierce, who climbed it a mere ten years after General Fremont's pronouncement of impossibility. Pierce came to Yreka during the Gold Rush and prospered as a miner and merchant. He was elected to represent Shasta County in the California Legislature of 1851–1852 and, while a member, introduced successful legislation to create Siskiyou County, wherein Mt. Shasta is located. During the summer of 1853 he was employed as an agent for the Yreka Water Company that provided water to the flourishing gold mines and sawmills. Earlier that year the company began construction on the Yreka Ditch, a canal to bring water from Parks Creek and the Shasta River north to Yreka for placer mining. Much of the canal remains today and can be seen clearly from high on Mt. Shasta contouring the west side of Shasta Valley.

The mountain thus was a familiar sight to Pierce, and it was not long before he began entertaining thoughts of climbing it. Pierce recollected in his memoirs: "I had made a statement that I believed I could make the trip to the loftiest peak, and some of my friends at Yreka put me to the test."

Pierce's climbing party, totaling seven, left Yreka on August 12, 1854, with provisions and a silk flag, and camped near the timberline on Shasta's northwest slope. Pierce's accounts of the climb accurately describe such landmarks as Misery Hill, the summit snowfield, and the sulphur fumaroles—features common to the conclusion of several climbing routes. But the description of his route on the lower slopes of the mountain is vague. Apparently his party ascended Cascade Gulch from the west, crossed the steep upper snowfields of the Whitney Glacier, then reached the summit before descending via Avalanche Gulch to the southwest.

Elias D. Pierce, credited with the first ascent of Mt. Shasta on August 14, 1854.

COURTESY SISKIYOU COUNTY MUSEUM

•

Fortunately for Pierce and his companions, these routes are two of Mt. Shasta's easiest—they are safely ascended each year by hundreds of climbers with the proper experience and equipment. Pierce and his group, however, were inexperienced mountaineers, and they encountered some frightful moments:

In climbing from one cliff to another, had we made one misstep, we would have gone headlong over a perpendicular precipice a thousand feet to the base. In many places we had to crawl over and around rough, craggy rocks, in single file, each one taking care of himself. In many places we had to raise our entire weight from one cliff of rocks to another. At length we succeeded in getting over this hazardous point or divide, after which we stopped to rest and view the fearful precipice we had just passed over. By cutting steps in the snow about three feet apart, we succeeded in getting over this difficult place by using our flag staff to assist each other in climbing.

They crossed the summit plateau, passed the noxious sulphur springs, and made the easy scramble up the summit crag:

> The day was calm, clear and serene, scarcely a breath of air stirring, and what little there was seemed so light that it was with the greatest difficulty that one could breathe. We climbed the eastern peak and took a survey of all below—there didn't appear to be anything above. Larger mountains that we were familiar with looked like small mole hills. All the scenery beneath was the most beautiful that my eyes ever looked upon. About 2 o'clock we planted the Stars and Stripes on the summit of Shasta Butte; and after lettering the face of a smooth, flat stone with a cold-chisel the year, day and date, we left the flag floating in the breeze, and began the descent on the same route as far as the snow plain. We all began to realize that the victory was ours, and as we were getting into our natural element began to feel much better.

THE DATE WAS AUGUST 14, 1854.

Pierce's party's success was not believed by the skeptical public, who still thought Mt. Shasta was impossible to climb. Pierce therefore organized a second ascent to prove his claims, and on September 19, 1854, nine climbers, led by Pierce, stood on Shasta's summit. Pierce succinctly commented after his second climb,

> There was no longer any doubt of the accessibility of the summit of Shasta Butte; although should one stand at its base and view its rugged form and towering peak, they would readily pronounce its ascent impossible.

John McKee, a member of the party, wrote a long, glowing account of the climb that appeared in *Beadle's Monthly Magazine,* one of the first accounts of an American big-mountain adventure to reach the public.

The veil of impossibility had been lifted from Mt. Shasta, and other ascents quickly followed Pierce's two climbs. The first solo ascent was made October 11, 1855, by Israel Diehl, a zealous temperance crusader who toured Northern California organizing Sons of Temperance chapters. Diehl estimated the height of the mountain to be between 16,000 and 17,000 feet and the peak to be "decidedly the most magnificent of our Union, if not of the continent."

The fifth ascent of Mt. Shasta was made on March 26, 1856, by a party of three led by Anton Roman. This climb was notable because it was made so early in the year. June, July, and August are the best months to climb Shasta—there's plenty of consolidated snow for smooth climbing, the days are long, and the weather is usually stable. A climb in March often has harsh, winterlike conditions.

Roman's trio did indeed encounter severe conditions; his thermometer was indicating twelve degrees below zero when he dropped and lost it in the snow, and he was forced to wrap his feet in strips of blanket to keep warm. Soon after the climb, Roman opened a bookstore in San Francisco that became a gathering place for many famous authors of the West, including Mark Twain, Charles Warren Stoddard, Ina Coolbrith, Thomas Starr King, and Bret Harte. When he began publishing *Overland Monthly,* a magazine that later featured several stories about Mt. Shasta, Bret Harte became its first editor. In 1875 Roman told Captain A. F. Rogers of the U.S. Coast and Geodetic Survey (which was soon to erect the Mt. Shasta summit monument), that he never entirely recovered from his freezing ordeal on Shasta's summit.

The first woman to climb Mt. Shasta was Olive Paddock Eddy, one of the pioneer residents of Shasta Valley, for whom

Olive Paddock Eddy

was the first woman to climb Mt. Shasta.

Mrs. Eddy, a prominent Siskiyou resident, made several later ascents.

COURTESY SISKIYOU COUNTY MUSEUM

•

nearby Mt. Eddy is named. Elias Pierce led a group of five women and seven men to the summit on September 9, 1856, in celebration of California's Admission Day. On the descent, the women were lowered one by one with ropes over the steep parapets of the Red Banks. That summer the Yreka Ditch water enterprise went bankrupt, leaving Pierce penniless. Soon after his third Shasta climb, Pierce left for Idaho, and he never returned to the mountain.

The first attempt to measure the height of Mt. Shasta was by William Moses on August 21, 1861. Moses, president of the Board of Trustees of Yreka, was accompanied by five other people, including Noah Brooks, editor of the *Marysville Appeal* and later a prominent writer on American politics. Moses had barometric instruments loaned to him by the Smithsonian Institute to take a reading of Shasta's summit elevation—a figure that had been debated since the discovery of the mountain.

He remained on the summit for several hours taking observations while his companions amused themselves reading the old newspapers and scribbled notes left by previous climbing parties. According to Moses's calculations, the height of Mt. Shasta was "a little less than 14,000 feet"—or, to be exact, 13,905 feet. This was a remarkably accurate determination when compared with Shasta's actual height of 14,162 feet, computed many years later. When Moses's height was announced (newspapers erroneously reported the height as 13,995 feet), it was greeted with ridicule from all sides, for it was commonly believed that the summit was several thousand feet higher. The *San Francisco Journal* reported:

> Altitude of Mt. Shasta: Mr. W. S. Moses, of Yreka, who has been making immense preparations to measure Mt. Shasta, has made out the altitude to be only 13,995. Nonsense, Mr. Moses, you have been using a last year's almanac. The altitude of Mount Shasta is nearer 19,000 feet.

The *Marysville Appeal* replied:

> A great deal you know about it, Mr. *Journal.* We have been there and swear that the altitude is only 13,995, by the Holy Moses!

By the 1880s there were three routes to Shasta's summit. The oldest and most popular one was from the southwest via Horse Camp—still the most frequented climbing route on Mt. Shasta. Another route, that went from Horse Camp to Shastina, then up the Whitney Glacier to the summit, was pioneered by local guide Justin Sisson, but rarely used. The gentle slope above Clear Creek on the mountain's southeast side was popular for its ease and became known as the "Stewart Trail" after Ed Stewart, one of Sisson's mountain guides. In 1883 Gilbert Thompson, a geographer with the U.S. Geological Survey, and

Guide Tom Watson (foreground) led Alice Cousins astride "Old Jump Up"

to the summit on September 23, 1903. This was the first horse to reach

Shasta's summit, and the picture was used in "Ripley's Believe It Or Not"

newspaper features for many years. EDWARD STUHL COLLECTION

·34·

local guide Tom Watson took two mules to the summit via the Stewart Trail. In 1903 Tom Watson guided Alice Cousins to the summit astride Old Jump Up, the first horse to reach the top. A photograph of the group at the summit was featured for years in "Ripley's Believe It or Not" cartoons.

Climbing Mt. Shasta eventually became somewhat more common and was no longer reserved exclusively for brave, adventurous "mountain men." Each summer increasing numbers of gentlemen in coats and women in full skirts—all wearing hobnailed boots and carrying long alpenstocks—made the summit climb. Mountaineering on Shasta was still unusual and interesting enough, however, to warrant newspaper coverage whenever a climb was attempted. Typical of the reports was this paragraph in the August 11, 1866, *Yreka Journal:*

> Several persons have undertaken to make the ascent of Mt. Shasta lately, but so far have failed on account of slippery crust on the snow. Some of those attempting the trip were badly scorched and blinded in the face by the reflection of the sun upon the snow.

During the 1860s, 1870s, and 1880s Mt. Shasta and the surrounding area became a popular tourist destination for climbers, as well as hunters and fishers. Strawberry Valley, the verdant bottom land stretching from today's Dunsmuir to Weed, attracted permanent settlers, some of whom began to provide board, lodging, and guide services for the growing numbers of tourists. Justin Sisson, famous for his tavern and knowledge of the mountain, was one of the first business people catering specifically to climbers. Many years before the railroad, regular stagecoach service arrived daily from Redding and the Sacramento Valley to disgorge passengers who had been lured by travel brochures describing Mt. Shasta as one of the marvels of California, if not the world. By the close of the nineteenth century, Mt. Shasta had become one of the most famous mountains in North America.

1890s climbers at Lake Helen, elevation 10,400 feet, on the popular

Avalanche Gulch climbing route. Note the blackened faces for protection from the sun.

EDWARD STUHL COLLECTION

A large group of climbers just below the Red Banks.

EDWARD STUHL COLLECTION

1890s climbers with long alpenstocks glissading down

the snow slopes above Lake Helen.

COURTESY SISKIYOU COUNTY MUSEUM

·36·

"Shaste Peak" by Alfred Agate, 1841. The first published picture of Mt. Shasta, painted during the United States Exploring Expedition of 1838–42.

CHAPTER 4

Scientific Exploration on Mt. Shasta

THE WILKES EXPEDITION

The United States in the nineteenth century was infused with energy and curiosity—attributes that launched the young American economy on a course of unrivaled expansion. With much of the initial discovery of the American West accomplished by the mid-1840s, economic goals became national political objectives. Professional explorers and scientists took to the field to assess and inventory the West's wealth of natural resources, contend with problems of mapping and transportation, and study Native American cultures, so vastly different from their own.

The first attempt at any scientific study of Mt. Shasta occurred during the United States's initial foray into global exploration. In 1828 Congress, encouraged by President John Quincy Adams, passed a resolution authorizing a special expedition to the Pacific. New England merchants, eager to find new whaling and sealing grounds and other commercially exploitable resources, had persuaded the government to sponsor a South Seas exploration.

The U.S. Navy welcomed the opportunity to explore new regions and "show the flag," and demonstrate to Europe that the young United States could mount and sustain a major venture overseas. On August 18, 1838, six ships under the command of Lieutenant Charles Wilkes left Hampton Roads, Virginia, on a round-the-world voyage that lasted four years. The United

States Exploring Expedition of 1838–1842, as it came to be known, returned with so many artifacts, specimens, and reports gathered by its crew of civilian scientists that the fledgling Smithsonian Institution, which accepted them, became the national museum of the United States.

After adventurous journeys to West Africa, South America, and the Antarctic continent, the Wilkes expedition explored several South Pacific archipelagoes before reaching the Hawaiian Islands in late September 1840. In July 1841 Wilkes sailed from Hawaii to the Columbia River in the Oregon Territory, whereupon one of his ships was wrecked on the bar at the river's mouth. Although the crew was rescued, many valuable collections and notes were lost. While a new ship was being outfitted, Wilkes conducted surveys and explorations through-out the Oregon Territory. He then sent a party led by Lieutenant George Emmons overland through California (then still part of Mexico) to San Francisco, where the entire expedition was reunited.

On September 29, 1841, Lieutenant Emmons and his group caught their first sight of Mt. Shasta from a gap in the Siskiyou mountains near today's California-Oregon border. Charles Wilkes's postexpedition report praised the view:

> The Shaste Peak is a magnificent sight, rising as it does to a lofty height, its steep sides emerging from the mists which envelope its base, and seem to throw it off to an immense distance; its cleft summit gave proof of its former active state as a volcano.

1849 engraving from a sketch of Mt. Shasta drawn by Wilkes Expedition

geologist James D. Dana on October 3, 1841.

COURTESY SMITHSONIAN INSTITUTION

The decision to send an overland contingent through California was undoubtedly politically motivated—intelligence gathered about the West Coast was of great importance to the American government as it negotiated for these lands in ensuing years—but it also allowed the scientists their first look at the Cascade peaks.

Expedition scientist James Dana was one of the most influential geologists of the nineteenth century and America's first volcanologist. He was able to study the Cascade volcanoes, especially Mt. Shasta, and was the first geologist to recognize the different Cascade volcanoes' similarities to Mt. Vesuvius— then a very recent volcano. Dana's *Geology,* published after the Wilkes expedition, offered new theories on different types of volcanoes and the processes by which they formed. His "explosion-collapse" theory explained the formation of large calderas, or craters, and rifts, such as Diller Canyon on Shastina's west flank, which Dana had observed when his party passed by Mt. Shasta.

William Brackenridge, the expedition botanist, discovered a previously unknown plant in the area and named it after William Darlington, who was then dean of American botanists. *Darlingtonia californica,* or California Pitcher Plant, is an unusual insect-eating plant found only in limited areas of Northern California and Oregon. A secretion from the plant's leaves attracts insects, which fall into a tubular lower portion, where they are digested. The plant was considered the expedition's best botanical find. Expedition scientists also collected the first specimens of Port Orford cedar. Asa Gray, a famous American botanist who organized much of the Wilkes botanical collection for the Smithsonian, was so impressed with the Shasta finds that he later journeyed to Mt. Shasta with John Muir for his own botanical studies.

During the time that Wilkes's overland party was encamped at the foot of Mt. Shasta, they saw large herds of antelope and mountain sheep and measured huge sugar pines. These behe-

The California Pitcher Plant, an insect-eating plant found near the base of Mt.

Shasta by Wilkes Expedition botanist William Brackenridge.

COURTESY SMITHSONIAN INSTITUTION

moth trees were found to be over eighteen feet in circumference, with cones sixteen inches long. Artist-naturalist Titian Peale described the expedition's upper Sacramento River canyon campsite, near today's town of Mount Shasta:

> We saw many fine springs, and in one of them a new species of Saracenia was found with leaves one or two feet long, besides a greater variety of singular plants than we have yet seen. It was a botanic harvest. . . . The summits of Mount Tchasty presented a beautiful view from our camp when its snow was illuminated by the pink rays of the setting sun, while the base remained invisible to us.

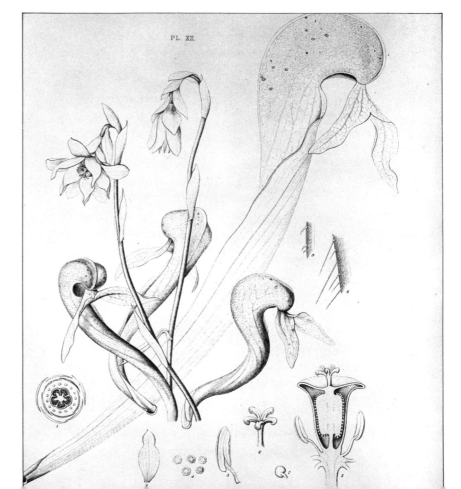

PL. XII.

Here, expedition artist Alfred Agate painted a picture of Mt. Shasta that became, in 1844, the first printed rendering of the mountain.

The Wilkes expedition's encounter with Mt. Shasta was more accidental than planned, for the group really had nothing more than a vague idea of the mountain's existence in the large, and barely known, Cascade range of volcanoes. However, important discoveries and observations were made near Mt. Shasta that influenced the history of the area. Wilkes's "Map of the Oregon Territory," published in 1844, was the most detailed map of the region at that time, and the first map to attach the name Shasta (by any of several spellings) to the mountain. General John C. Fremont relied heavily on Wilkes's maps in preparing his own maps of the much greater trans-Mississippi West. Fremont's widely distributed maps were largely responsible for popular acceptance of the name and location of Mt. Shasta.

Another important work of the expedition was the gathering of Native American cultural and linguistic information. Horatio Hale, the expedition ethnographer, published the first Native American language studies of the area—information that later helped identify some of the possible sources of the "Shasta" name.

Although the Wilkes expedition remained near Mt. Shasta only about a week, the visit was significant. It was the first time trained scientists had focused their inquisitive minds on the mountain. Their reports and observations on natural history, cartography, and native cultures initiated a long and dedicated period of scientific attention to Mt. Shasta. Forty years afterward historian Hubert Bancroft wrote that the expedition's maps and studies were the first to authenticate the Pacific Northwest:

> These shores, which hitherto were little more than myths in the world's mind, were now clothed in reality.

JOSIAH WHITNEY AND THE CALIFORNIA GEOLOGICAL SURVEY

In December 1848, shortly after the initial Gold Rush to California began, geologist Josiah Dwight Whitney, who had been conducting surveys of the Lake Superior copper region, wrote to his brother William:

> California is all the rage now and poor Lake Superior has to be shoved into the background. We are already planning to secure the geological survey of that interesting land, where the farmers can't plough their fields by reason of the huge lumps of gold in the soil!

The geography of California was a large and complex entity with little known of the potential resources of the land. Whitney noted, "In 1860, California was, geologically speaking, an unknown land." To remedy this situation, California Governor John Downey authorized a bill on April 21, 1860, creating the office of State Geologist to make an accurate and complete geologic survey of the state with special attention to mineral resources. Whitney, chosen for the position, was experienced in metallurgy and chemistry, as well as geology, and was strongly recommended by the highest scientific circles in the country. His assistant, William H. Brewer, was equally qualified.

During the winter of 1860–1861 Whitney's group began the survey in Southern California. For most of 1861 they surveyed the Salinas Valley in central California, then followed the Sacramento River north to Strawberry Valley at the foot of Mt. Shasta in September 1862. As they made preparations to climb the peak, Brewer commented on the dearth of information available on the mountain:

The California Geological Survey's field party of 1864.

William Brewer is seated; Clarence King is standing at the right.

Assistants James Gardiner and Richard Cotter are at the left.

COURTESY BANCROFT LIBRARY

Here let me say that Mt. Shasta is the highest point in the State, that it has long been an object of admiration and wonder, that it has been ascended by a number of persons, and yet absolutely nothing was known of it except its existence—of its geology and structure not a word can be found anywhere; of its height, matters were nearly as vague.

On September 12, 1862, Whitney and Brewer climbed Mt. Shasta from the southwest side by today's popular Avalanche Gulch route and obtained several barometric readings at the summit to compute an altitude of 14,440 feet. They also carefully studied the variety of lavas to identify Shasta as a volcano of the Tertiary period in geologic time and reported that in spite of immense snowfall, no glaciers formed on the mountain. Brewer recalled his experiences on Shasta:

> Many told us that it was an impossibility to reach the highest summit—some on account of ice, some because of sulphurous vapors, some because of its steepness, etc. Such were the stories, a few grains of truth, and an abundance of pure fiction. When we got to the top we found people had been there before us. There was a liberal distribution of 'California conglomerate,' a mixture of tin cans and broken bottles, a newspaper, a Methodist hymnbook, a pack of cards, an empty bottle, and various other evidences of a bygone civilization.

Whitney lacked the time and equipment to make a thorough survey of the mountain, but his elevation measurements established an accepted scientific figure for Shasta's height. In December 1862 he made a formal presentation to the California Academy of Natural Sciences, where he expressed his belief that Mt. Shasta was the highest mountain in the United States. Whitney's calculation of a height of 14,440 feet supported

William Moses's figure of 13,905 feet made in 1861, a measurement that had been scoffed at since it was popularly believed that the elevation of Mt. Shasta was somewhere between 15,000 and 20,000 feet. Whitney's august scientific reputation made his measurement the bona fide one, although it was often reported as a fancier-appearing 14,444 feet in travel articles.

CLARENCE KING

Upon his return to Strawberry Valley after the Mt. Shasta climb, William Brewer wrote a letter to an old friend, George Jarvis Brush, Professor of Metallurgy at Yale University, describing in glowing terms his experiences on Shasta. Shortly after Brush received the correspondence, one of his students, Clarence King, happened by Brush's office and read Brewer's account. For the mercurial King, who would eventually rise to the directorship of the U.S. Geological Survey, this was a pivotal moment. Yale geology professor James Dana supplemented Brewer's descriptions with his own recollections of the Wilkes expedition.

King had become fascinated with large mountains and glaciers through study under Louis Agassiz, a distinguished scientist famous for his European glacial studies and ice-age theories. The description of Mt. Shasta made up his mind. He immediately volunteered as an assistant field geologist, without pay, to Whitney's ongoing California survey. King was not disappointed in his first encounter with the mountain. He wrote:

"At last, through a notch to the northward, rose the conical summit of Shasta, its pale, rosy lavas enamelled with ice. From that moment the peak became the centre of our life."

While doing field work on Shasta's slopes during the summer of 1864, Brewer and King discovered an unusual milky looking stream, not unlike the silty runoff a glacier would produce. Brewer remarked that if it were in Switzerland, he would consider it a typical glacier-fed stream. King asked his companion why not this one, and Brewer replied that he had been on Shasta's upper snowfields in 1862 without discovering any glacial ice or crevasses. Evidence of an ancient glacial epoch along California's interior mountain ranges had already been recognized, but leading American glaciologists and geologists—including Josiah Whitney, James Dana, and Louis Agassiz—were certain that no *active* glaciers remained anywhere in the United States.

The mystery was not to be solved until King returned to Mt. Shasta in the fall of 1870. His success on Whitney's California survey had led, with helpful recommendations from Professors Dana and Agassiz, to directorship of the government-sponsored Geologic Survey of the Fortieth Parallel. This survey concentrated on mineral deposits centered on the fortieth parallel of the western United States, approximately the line of the Union

September 11, 1870. Carleton Watkins' original photograph of Clarence King at the edge of Shasta's Whitney Glacier, the first active glacier discovered and photographed in the United States. COURTESY USGS

and Central Pacific railroads. King had also secured from the government special permission to study volcanoes along the Pacific Coast.

When King climbed Mt. Shasta in September 1870, he ascended it from the northwest via the immense saddle between Shasta and Shastina. Accompanied by assistants, including the pioneer Yosemite photographer Carleton Watkins, he bivouacked on the Shastina crater rim and got the first view of an active glacier in the United States—Shasta's great northside ice river. Many years later he told Brewer, "That stream haunted me for years, until I got on Mt. Shasta and found the glaciers."

The great upper Whitney Glacier photographed by Carleton Watkins from Shastina's rim. "Watkins pitched his field-tent for photographic work, and when he thought he had the light all shut-off, found that enough still came through the ice-floor to spoil his negatives, obliging him to cover the floor of the tent also."—Clarence King, September 11, 1870

King later named the glacier after his mentor, Josiah Whitney. He recorded the moment in his journal:

> There, winding its huge body along, lay a
> glacier, riven with sharp, deep crevasses yawning
> fifty or sixty feet wide, the blue hollows of their
> shadowed depth contrasting with the brilliant
> surfaces of ice . . . while Watkins was making his
> photographic views, I climbed about, going to
> the edges of some crevasses and looking over
> into their blue vaults, where icicles overhang,
> and a whispered sound of waterflow comes
> faintly from beneath.

Watkins had laboriously packed his cumbersome cameras, glass photographic plates, and darkroom tent up the mountain and was rewarded with the chance to produce the first photographs of a glacier in America.

The next day King's party followed the upper glacier to Shasta's summit, where they spent another night. The weather was calm and clear, and King was transfixed by the view. He later wrote,

> So high is Shasta, so dominant above the
> field of view, we looked over it all as upon a grea
> shield which rose gently in all directions to the
> sky. What volumes of geographical history lay in
> view! Old mountain uplift; volcanoes built upon
> the plain of fiery lava; the chill of ice and wearing
> force of torrent, written in glacier-gorge and
> water-curved canyon."

King was baffled as to how every other scientific visitor to the mountain had overlooked its huge fields of ice. The puzzle solved itself when King and his party descended Shasta's south side, along the route of earlier climbers: "From the moment we left the summit we encountered less and less snow, and at no part of the journey were we able to see a glacier."

For several weeks after their descent, King and his assistants explored Shasta's flanks. As a result of these explorations, King announced the discovery of five active glaciers that had been hidden from Dana, Whitney, and Brewer. Their discovery excited King to such an extent that he sent his assistants to other Cascade peaks on a successful quest to look for similar ice fields. Of Shasta, he wrote:

> The discovery of active glaciers and the
> knowledge we have gotten of the volcanic period
> are among the most important late additions of
> American geology.

King was a gifted writer who skillfully combined science and aesthetics. His articulate and descriptive field notes and journals became the basis for a popular series of articles that appeared in the *Atlantic Monthly* and, later, in his book, *Mountaineering in the Sierra Nevada,* published in 1872. King humorously reminisced on his Shasta experiences in this poem:

> I've clum' 'mong alpine mountains
> And forest that's all pine too,
> I've drinkt at bitter fountains
> Whar some took whiskey in lieu.
> Not even all them postage stamps
> Left by the late J. Astor
> Would tempt this sorry child again
> To shin the cone of Shaster.
> I'll bet that old excelsior,
> For all he's reckoned limber,
> Couldn't dodge them rollin' rocks
> Nor shy that rottin' timber.

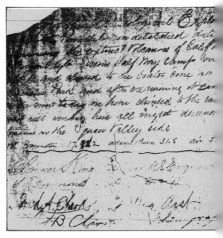

Original summit register dated September 12, 1870 from Clarence King's

Mt. Shasta climb: "Party of the U.S. Geological Exploration of Fortieth

Parallel on detached duty examining the extinct volcanoes of California . . ."

King's signature is first, followed by his assistants Emmons and Clark, and

photographer Carleton B. Watkins. COURTESY BANCROFT LIBRARY

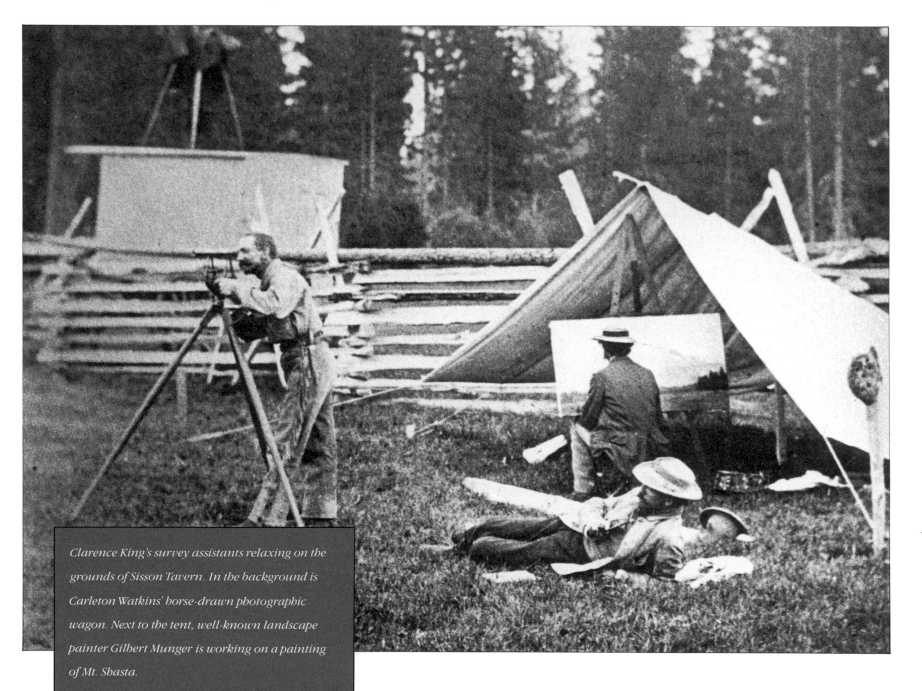

Clarence King's survey assistants relaxing on the grounds of Sisson Tavern. In the background is Carleton Watkins' horse-drawn photographic wagon. Next to the tent, well-known landscape painter Gilbert Munger is working on a painting of Mt. Shasta.

PHOTOGRAPH BY CARLETON WATKINS, COURTESY USGS

NAMING SHASTA'S GLACIERS

Unlike most explorers, Clarence King was not greatly concerned with bestowing names on every lake, river, and mountain he encountered. His field notes contained a reference to a "McCloud Glacier"—today's Konwakiton Glacier—on the mountain's south side, and he named the Whitney Glacier, but that was the extent of his interest in designating names. The credit for naming Mt. Shasta's other glaciers goes to the famous American explorer, Major John Wesley Powell.

Major Powell, the one-armed Civil War veteran best known for his daring voyage down the turbulent Colorado River in 1869, succeeded King as director of the U.S. Geological Survey. When Powell began his famous river exploration of the Grand Canyon country, the region was virtually unknown to white explorers. Although the expedition was primarily a geographic and geologic survey, Powell quickly recognized the inherent danger of distorting Native American history through contact with Euro-Americans. Powell was a brilliant scholar—a fact often eclipsed by his heroic exploits—and his ethnographic studies expanded into the U.S. Bureau of Ethnology, of which he became the first director.

Powell collected over two dozen language dictionaries of Western tribes and wrote several booklets on the study of Native American languages and dialects. During the fall of 1879 he came to Northern California specifically to study the Wintun tribe and successfully climbed Mt. Shasta on November 1, 1879. Powell returned to the area in 1880 to finish his studies of the Wintun and complete a dictionary of their language. During this trip he named Shasta's four other major glaciers with Wintun words in honor of the tribe he loved and respected: *Hotlum* ("steep," or "steep rock"); *Bolam* ("big," or "great"); *Konwakiton* ("muddy," or "mud creek"); and *Wintun* (the tribal name). These names were placed on official record by the U.S. Geographic Board in 1897.

·46·

A page from John Wesley Powell's field notebook of Wintun Indian words. Note "Kong-wa-ka-tong" for Mud Creek and "Hlot-lam" for Steep Rocks— words Powell used to name two of Shasta's glaciers.

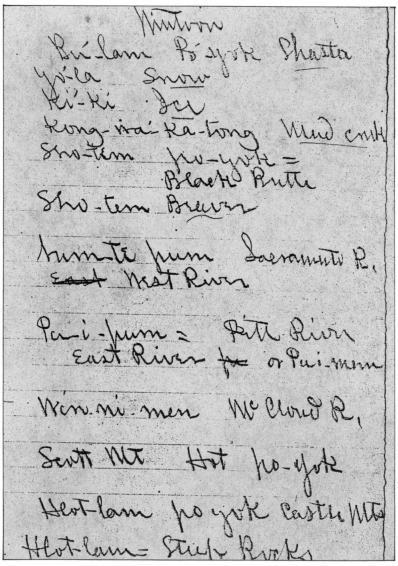

Explorer John Wesley Powell's summit register signature on November 1, 1879. Powell came to Mt. Shasta to study the local Native American culture.

Two of Shasta's northeast side glaciers named by John Wesley Powell in 1880.

The Wintum glacier is on the left; the Hotlum glacier is on the right.

1870 Carleton Watkins photograph. COURTESY USGS

Augustus Rodgers, Assistant Director of the U. S. Coast and Geodetic Survey, in charge of constructing a signal tower on Mt. Shasta's summit.

EDWARD STUHL COLLECTION

•

THE GEODETIC MONUMENT

In 1875 the U.S. Coast and Geodetic Survey became interested in installing a signal tower on the summit of Mt. Shasta to use as a fixed point in their West Coast surveys. Augustus Rodgers, a career civil servant in the survey's San Francisco office, was instructed to explore the feasibility of constructing a signal or beacon on the summit that could be seen from Mt. Saint Helena (near Clear Lake, California) and Mt. Lola (west of Reno, Nevada), mountains well south of Mt. Shasta that were included as part of the survey grid.

On April 28, 1875, Rodgers, along with John Muir and local guide Jerome Fay, climbed Mt. Shasta by today's popular Avalanche Gulch route. Two days later Muir and Fay climbed the

mountain again to take barometric measurements. A fierce storm caught the pair on the summit, and, unable to descend, they were forced to spend the night huddled over the summit's hot sulphur fumaroles, alternately scalded and frozen as they constantly shifted position. Muir's account of the extraordinary experience, "A Snow Storm on Mt. Shasta," was one of his most famous writings (see pages 65–66 for a further description of this episode).

Upon returning to San Francisco, Rodgers recommended that the Coast and Geodetic Survey erect on Shasta's summit an iron monument capped with a copper conoid, nickel-plated and polished to reflect the sun. The plan was immediately accepted, and the monument was fabricated in a San Francisco foundry. On September 28, 1875, the monument—its 3,500 pounds of material broken down into smaller, manageable sections—arrived at Strawberry Valley. Justin Sisson, the local innkeeper and guide, contracted with the survey to transport the monument to the summit in three stages; by wagon, horse, and finally Native American porters. By October 3 all the materials had been delivered to Shasta's summit, where Rodgers and his assistants remained for four days to assemble the iron tower. When completed, the monument measured almost fifteen feet from its base to the top of its reflecting conoid, and was two and a half feet in diameter. The hollow shaft was filled with broken rock for stability and the outer surface was painted black to protect the iron cylinder from rust.

Even though the autumn weather was relatively calm in Strawberry Valley, sustained cold temperatures, biting winds, and the constant effects of high altitude made the assembly of the monument an ordeal for Rodgers and his group. They were forced to anchor their canvas tents with large rocks and to melt snow over the hot springs for drinking and cooking water. Rodgers wrote: "It was sufficient incentive to constant hard work on the part of the men, in order to get through as quickly as possible." When they descended the mountain and returned to Sisson's tavern, Rodgers recalled that the monument was easily

The various designs for the summit signal tower.

The design on the right was the one chosen and erected on Mt. Shasta's summit during the fall of 1875.

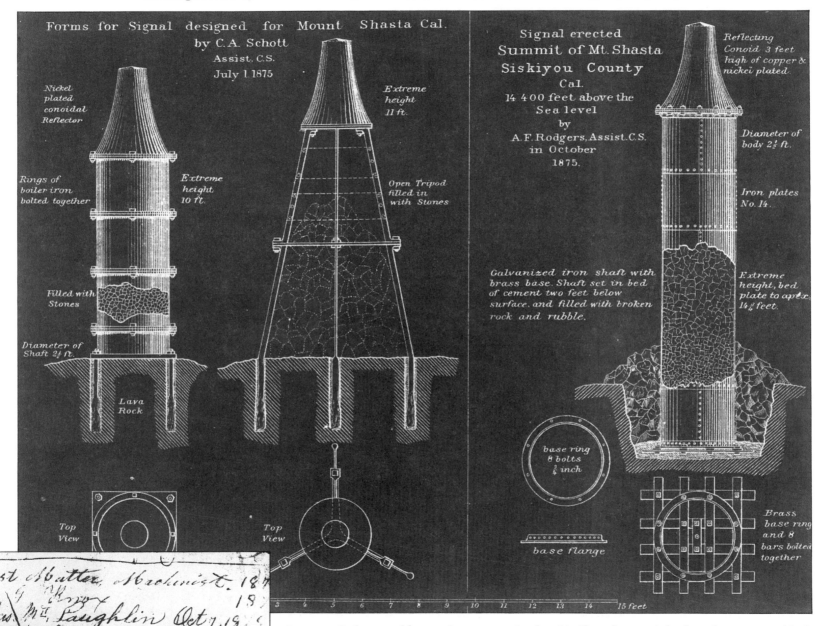

Forms for Signal designed for Mount Shasta Cal.
by C.A. Schott
Assist. C.S.
July 1. 1875

Nickel plated conoidal Reflector

Rings of boiler iron bolted together

Extreme height 10 ft.

Filled with Stones

Diameter of Shaft 2¼ ft.

Lava Rock

Top View

Extreme height 11 ft.

Open Tripod filled in with Stones

Top View

Signal erected Summit of Mt. Shasta Siskiyou County Cal.
14 400 feet above the Sea level
by
A.F. Rodgers, Assist. C.S.
in October 1875.

Galvanized iron shaft with brass base. Shaft set in bed of cement two feet below surface, and filled with broken rock and rubble.

base ring 8 bolts ¾ inch

base flange

Reflecting Conoid 3 feet high of copper & nickel plated.

Diameter of body 2½ ft.

Iron plates No. 14.

Extreme height, bed plate to apex, 14⅞ feet.

Brass base ring and 8 bars bolted together

3 4 5 6 7 8 9 10 11 12 13 14 15 feet

·49·

Augustus Rodgers and four assistants remained on Mt. Shasta's summit for four days to assemble the signal tower. "These are the 4 men who erected the signal post for the U. S. Coast Survey under the superintendent of Capt. A. F. Rodgers." Original summit register book. COURTESY BANCROFT LIBRARY

visible from Strawberry Valley and glistened in the sunlight like "a light-house tower with brilliant lamps burning." A week after the work was completed, snowfall covered the entire mountain.

In 1878 Coast and Geodetic Survey Director Carlisle P. Patterson authorized a well-known California geographer, Professor George Davidson, to place surveyors and equipment on Shasta's summit in order to conduct measurements utilizing the geodetic monument, then the highest signal tower ever used for geographic sightings. Survey assistant Benjamin Colonna was assigned the task and spent nine continuous days on the summit. Colonna's equipment, including a theodolite, for accurately measuring angles, and a heliostat, a polished surface for reflecting light, weighed more than 750 pounds and, like Rodgers' loads, had to be transported from the timberline to the summit by Native American porters.

On August 1 Colonna arose to an icy dawn and prepared his theodolite for viewing.

> At sunrise, I turned my telescope in the direction of Mount Lola, and there was the [heliostat], one hundred and sixty-nine miles off, shining like a star of the first magnitude. I gave a few flashes from my own, and they were at once answered by flashes from Lola. Then turning my telescope in the direction of Mount St. Helena, there, too, was a [heliostat], shining as prettily as the one at Lola! The line from Mount Shasta to Mount St. Helena is one hundred and ninety-two miles long, or twenty-three miles longer than their longest. And the glory is ours; for America, and not Europe, can boast of the largest trigonometrical figures that have ever been measured on the globe!

(The French had recently succeeded in measuring record terrestrial distances from Spain across the Mediterranean to Algiers—a distance of approximately 169 miles.)

When his observations were finished, Colonna lashed up his equipment and supplies in blankets and rolled them off the Red Banks, where they bounded and slid a vertical half-mile to Lake Helen. Colonna then tied a gunnysack around his waist and enjoyed the glissade down Avalanche Gulch, just as today's climbers do.

The U.S. Coast and Geodetic Survey was responsible for providing accurate charts of the coast and navigational hazards and in the spring of 1903 began plotting a new series of detailed maps and coastal charts covering central California to Puget Sound. During the summer of 1904 the latest and most accurate elevation of Mt. Shasta was determined. Observations from six fixed points on lesser mountains surrounding Mt. Shasta resulted in an elevation measurement of 4316.3 meters, or 14,162 feet, the figure accepted to this day. The primary arc of triangulation for the Coast and Geodetic Survey's new generation of maps—and Mt. Shasta's elevation—was calculated from Colonna's measurements from Shasta's summit.

After Colonna's survey work was completed, the monument was abandoned for any further scientific use. For many years it was customary for climbers to paint or scratch their names on the tower, and a can of white paint was even kept near the monument's base for that purpose. Then, in the fall of 1903, the monument collapsed from its summit pedestal, a victim of brutal winds and weather. For several years the whereabouts of the tower was unknown, until climbers found the crushed cylinder protruding from permanent snowfields at the west base of the summit pinnacle. The copper reflector was brought down in 1949 and can now be seen at the Sisson Museum in the town of Mount Shasta.

Another "observation" by a member of the U.S. Coast and Geodetic Survey arouses interest and debate to this day. Many Native American legends refer to seeing the ocean from the top of Mt. Shasta, and claims are still heard from climbers who are positive that they have seen the Pacific from the summit. Professor George Davidson, the geographer in charge of Colonna's observations from Mt. Shasta, was sure he saw the mountain through the gap of the Klamath River canyon while sailing down the Oregon and California coasts in 1886. Repeated claims over the years of sighting Mt. Shasta from the sea, or seeing the ocean from Shasta's summit, finally caused the U.S. Coast and Geodetic Survey to scientifically examine the possibilities. In 1928 the survey concluded that it was mathematically impossible to see Mt. Shasta from the ocean, or vice versa: a line from the summit, tangent to the ocean's surface, would be blocked by the coast range of mountains.

The graffiti-adorned summit monument in 1896.

EDWARD STUHL COLLECTION

·51·

THE U.S. GEOLOGICAL SURVEYS

Following Clarence King's pioneer geologic explorations on Mt. Shasta, several other scientific surveys studied the mountain in greater detail. In the summer of 1882 the U.S. Geological Survey (USGS) began a geologic and topographic study of the Cascade volcanoes of Northern California and Oregon. During 1883 and 1884, USGS geologist Joseph Diller made a thorough study of Mt. Shasta's geologic features and concluded that the mountain—as well as Mt. Lassen—belonged to the same geologic epoch as the northern Cascade volcanoes and therefore formed the southernmost members of the Cascade Range.

Diller studied Mt. Shasta's formation, various lavas, surface features, and the recently discovered glaciers and theorized that the Konwakiton Glacier was the only one of Shasta's glaciers to have left a prominent record of geologic change. He estimated it to have once been over 5 miles long, which explained the existence of huge Mud Creek Canyon on the mountain's south side. Diller, a dedicated scientist who served forty-one years with the USGS, was the first geologist dispatched to Mt. Lassen when it unexpectedly erupted in 1914 and the first to give a detailed account of the formation of southern Oregon's famous Crater Lake.

But it was Mt. Shasta that Diller considered to be the finest example of an isolated mountain built by volcanic forces. He was impressed by the primal qualities of Shasta and described the mountain in strong, basic terms:

> It has long been the field whereon was fought the battle between the elements within the earth and those above it. In the early days the forces beneath were victorious and built up the mountain in face of wind and weather, but gradually the volcanic energy reached its climax, declined, and passed away. Fiery lava has been succeeded by arctic cold.

Geologist Joseph Diller's excellent 1884 photograph of Mt. Shasta's east side. The Konwakiton Glacier is at the left; the Wintun Glacier is at the extreme right; the Watkins Glacier is the small oblong snowfield right of center. Mud Creek is at the left and Clear Creek is at right-center.

COURTESY USGS

*Gilbert Thompson's original summit register entry when he and guide
Tom Watson brought two mules to the top of Mt. Shasta in 1883.*

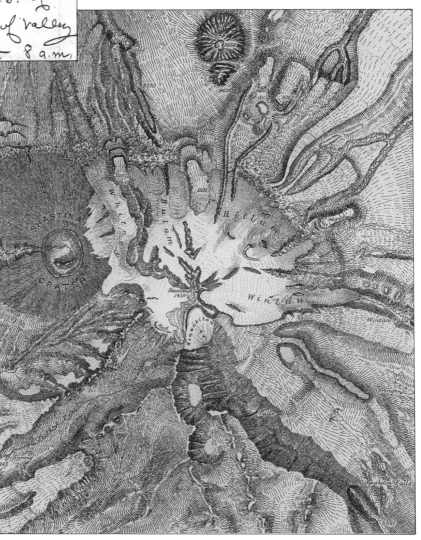

·53·

*USGS topographer Gilbert Thompson's 1883 map of Mt. Shasta showed
various climbing and exploration routes as well as physical features.
The dashed "hachure" marks were a predecessor to contour lines
which came into use the following year.*

At the same time that Diller was studying Shasta's geology and volcanology, Gilbert Thompson, also of the USGS, was conducting a topographic survey of the mountain. Thompson measured the size of Shasta's five known glaciers, took barometric altitude readings at the summit and other prominent landmarks, and named several of the mountain's major features, including Shastina, Mt. Shasta's large secondary cone. He also located and studied some smaller snow and ice fields, overlooked in comparison to Shasta's major glaciers, and believed that they might also qualify as glaciers—a conclusion born out many years later. During Thompson's field surveys, he and local guide Tom Watson led two mules, Dynamite and Croppie, to Shasta's summit on September 10, 1883. Thompson was very proud of the accomplishment of leading mules to the summit and kept a shoe worn by one of the animals on his Washington, D.C. desk for the remainder of his government career.

For the next two summers USGS work was continued on Mt. Shasta by Eugene Ricksecker and Mark Kerr, who completed the survey with a detailed "Mount Shasta Quadrangle" map. This map was used as the basis for a large model of the mountain shown at the New Orleans Exposition and the National Museum in Washington, D.C. In keeping with the cartographic practices of the time, Gilbert Thompson's topographic maps of Shasta indicated heights and depths by means of *hachure marks*—short lines used to indicate slope and direction—a method more artistic than geographically accurate. Ricksecker's and Kerr's map incorporated the first use of detailed *contour lines* to portray the topography of the mountain.

Information from Joseph Diller's geologic studies of Mt. Shasta was added to Eugene Ricksecker's 1884 topographic map and published by the USGS in 1895 as the "Shasta Special Map." Contour lines had replaced hachure marks.

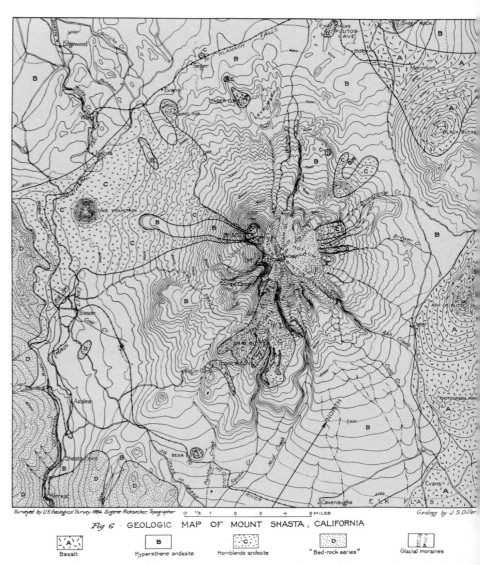

Fig 6 · GEOLOGIC MAP OF MOUNT SHASTA, CALIFORNIA

Basalt — Hypersthene andesite — Hornblende andesite — "Bed-rock series" — Glacial moraines

Fig. 6. The topography of Mount Shasta is published by the Geological Survey on the scale of 1:62500 as "Shasta Special Map." With additions, but on a smaller scale, the American Book Co., in New York published it in 1895 as No. 8, p. 246, of a series of National Geographic Monographs under the title, Mount Shasta, a Typical Volcano.

Polygonum Shastense.
Shasta Knotweed

w. Stuhl

The Shasta Knotweed, first discovered by William Brewer on the California

Geological Survey. Watercolor by Edward Stuhl.

BIOLOGIC STUDIES

Mt. Shasta's immense geologic presence naturally attracted the attention of physical scientists—geologists, volcanologists, cartographers, and geographers—but by no means was the mountain's biologic history neglected. Geographically, the mountain occupies a unique position, appearing at the hub of three separate ranges: the Sierra Nevada to the southeast, the Cascade Range to the north, and the Klamath Mountains, immediately westward across Strawberry Valley. Shasta's proximity to these ranges, while still standing alone, has always attracted the attention of scientists interested in plant and animal distribution on the mountain.

The very earliest botanical studies were carried out by the Wilkes expedition, which discovered several new plant species during its traverses of the upper Sacramento Valley in 1841. The famous British botanist John Jeffrey explored Mt. Shasta's slopes in 1852, making the first field notes on the habitat of the white-bark pine, which he found as high as 9,000 feet. A few weeks later he discovered the pine that now bears his name, the Jeffrey pine, in Shasta Valley. William Brewer collected scores of plants—many previously undescribed—during his explorations with Josiah Whitney on the California Geological Survey in 1862. During that trip Whitney found a small grove of spruce with long, pendant branches and gave a specimen to Brewer. Twenty years later the rare tree was named the Brewer, or Weeping, spruce. And Professor Asa Gray, who had organized the Wilkes expedition's botanical specimens for the Smithsonian Institution, traveled to Mt. Shasta with John Muir in 1877, where they were awed by the mountain's beautiful stands of Shata red fir.

One of the most thorough biologic studies made on Mt. Shasta was the U.S. Department of Agriculture's survey in 1898 by Dr. C. Hart Merriam. Merriam is best know for developing the "Life-Zone" theory, a generalized classification of plant and animal distribution according to elevation and climatic factors. (His terms *Upper Sonoran, Transition, Canadian, Hudsonian,* and *Alpine* are very familiar to biology students.)

One of Merriam's first field applications of his zonal theory took place on the 1898 Mt. Shasta biologic survey. During the survey, Merriam and his assistants made the first timberline circumnavigation of the mountain. He completed the first systematic study of Shasta's life forms and revealed the fact that although the mountain was definitely part of the Cascade chain of peaks, its plant and animal life was related more closely to the northern Sierra. Merriam knew from previous field studies that many plant and animal species were common to both the Sierra Nevada and Cascade Range; he thought Shasta's unique geographical position, overlapping the two mountain ranges, would provide an abundance of species from each area.

However, Shasta was much drier, concluded Merriam, than either the Sierra or the Cascades, and many species common to the two ranges were absent. There were also many species found only on Mt. Shasta. Merriam identified over a dozen new plant and animal species, and many of these have been given the name Shastensis, or Shasta, in their scientific descriptions. For example, Shasta red fir (*Abies magnifica var. shastensis*), Shasta knotweed, and Shasta bluebell. Many plant species have their "type location" on Mt. Shasta. That is, although they occur elsewhere, they were first discovered on the mountain.

Other plants have borrowed the named "Shasta" while being completely foreign to the mountain's slopes. The Shasta daisy, an attractive flower bred by the famous American horticulturist Luther Burbank, was thus named because he was impressed by Shasta's snow-covered vista. (At one time this daisy was promoted as the United States' national flower.)

Dr. C. Hart Merriam's plant studies excited Dr. William Bridge Cooke, who began a long association with Mt. Shasta

when he came to the mountain in 1936 to collect specimens for one of his college professors. Over the following years Cooke studied and collected flowering plants, ferns, mosses, and fungi, and published the comprehensive *Flora of Mt. Shasta* in 1940. It, together with several supplements, lists more than five hundred species of flowering plants and more than six hundred species of fungi.

Merriam opined at the end of the nineteenth century that Shasta's unique location among the Sierra, Cascade, and Klamath ranges would always make it a treasure-trove for plant geographers:

> All high mountains, particularly those that stand alone, are likely to throw light on the problems of geographic distribution and are worthy of careful study. Shasta, not only because of its great altitude, but even more because of its intermediate position between the Sierra and the Cascades.

Looking down Diller Canyon from the rim of Shastina. This great cleft in Shastina's west flank was named by C. Hart Merriam during his timberline circumnavigation of Mt. Shasta in 1898.
1870 Photograph by Carleton Watkins. COURTESY USGS

Cooke found that some of Merriam's life zones were unusually indistinct on Shasta, and in some isolated cases, even reversed. For example, Cooke found chaparral fields above the usual timberline trees on Shasta's north side and an unusual grove of quaking aspen on Shastina's northwest shoulder. He also discovered the diminutive Phacelia cookei, a flower found nowhere else in the world. Even in his later years, Cooke con-tinued to visit Mt. Shasta each summer to collect specimens and gather information on botanical and mycological distributions. (He died in December 1991.)

Dr. William Bridge Cooke, Mt. Shasta's premiere botanist, at the Shasta Alpine Lodge in the 1940s. Dr. Cooke was Lodge custodian during the late 1930s and early 1940s.

Merriam's Arnica, found by Dr. C. Hart Merriam at Squaw Valley Meadows on Shasta's east side. Watercolor by Edward Stuhl.

COURTESY MERIAM LIBRARY

RECENT EXPLORATION

The era of scientific exploration on Mt. Shasta is by no means complete. Scientists continue to initiate studies and make new discoveries on the mountain's slopes. Since the catastrophic eruption of Mt. St. Helens in 1980, the USGS has been carefully monitoring the Cascade volcanoes. Mt. Shasta's glacial ice and snow volume has been surveyed and estimated, and its seismic activity has been monitored and recorded for eruption-

hazard analyses and planning. Any volcanic activity on Mt. Shasta has the potential to unleash massive glacier melt, floods, and mud flows from the mountain's estimated five *billion* cubic feet of snow and ice.

In 1924 a large quantity of ice broke off from the Konwaki-ton Glacier and lodged at the bottom of Mud Creek Canyon, forming a dam. Water and mud collected for a month, then burst through, forming a plain of glacial debris 5 to 6 miles long and over a mile wide. Mud and boulders closed roads, including Highway 89 near McCloud. Mud poured into Sacramento River

The lower Whitney Glacier, scene of outburst floods that travelled more than 10 miles in 1985. 1870 photograph by Carleton Watkins.

COURTESY USGS

A NEW CHANNEL 40 FT DEEP CUT BY "MUD CREEK" McCLOUD. CAL. 1924

U. S. FOREST SERVICE

McCLOUD RIVER RY TRAIN STALLED IN FLOW FROM "MUD CREEK. 1924

U. S. FOREST SERVICE

tributaries and silted the water as far as San Francisco Bay. In July 1985 several consecutive days of unusually hot weather triggered "jokulhlaups," or outburst floods, from the Whitney Glacier, which caused severe road and property damage more than 10 miles downstream.

The University of Chicago has been studying Shasta's lower Hotlum Glacier since 1976, measuring and charting its annual movement. The results and conclusions of the study are not yet published, but the university's long interest in the mountain has resulted in the Hotlum Glacier's small, but very active and separate northern lobe being considered by the USGS to be named Chicago Glacier on new maps.

Two amateur geologists recently demonstrated that Mt. Shasta's glacial history required some additions, verifying Gilbert Thompson's 1883 prediction that additional, small glaciers might still be found. Harry Watkins, who resided for many years in McCloud and Mount Shasta, was intrigued with the post-1940s apparent resurgence of Shasta's glaciers and found a small glacier on the mountain's east side in the 1950s. Watkins took comparative photographs of the glacier for many years to substantiate its existence. The small glacier, located at the head of the large Clear Creek basin, was named in honor of Watkins, who died only a few years before the glacier officially appeared on USGS maps. Another small glacier was identified on Mt. Shasta's southeast flank by geologist Phil Rhodes in the early 1980s. This glacier, just west of the Konwakiton Glacier, was named the Mud Creek Glacier.

As the century draws to a close, our planet Earth is beginning to experience climatic changes, weather extremes, and other symptoms of the "greenhouse effect." Mt. Shasta, because of its distinct weather patterns, active glaciers, and solitary location, will continue to be studied for micro- and macrogeologic and biologic clues; what we learn on Shasta and other large mountains can be a bellweather to upcoming changes on our planet.

·59·

Late 1880s Yreka gold miner.

COURTESY PETER PALMQUIST

CHAPTER 5

MOUNTAIN PEOPLE

JUSTIN SISSON

STRAWBERRY VALLEY, THE MEADOWLAND WHERE THE PRESENT TOWN OF MOUNT SHASTA IS LOCATED, WAS NAMED BY EARLY TRAVELERS THROUGH THE AREA FOR ITS ABUNDANCE OF WILD STRAWBERRIES. From 1854 to 1886 the first townsite was called Berryvale, then changed to Sisson, after Justin Sisson, the renowned innkeeper who was the area's first guide and postmaster.

Sisson was attracted to Northern California by the Gold Rush, but instead fell in love with Strawberry Valley and disregarded the lure of gold. He and his wife, Lydia, spent the winter of 1861 in a log cabin, then a few years later bought a large house and converted the upstairs rooms for paying guests. William Sullaway, from whom Sisson bought the house, operated a stage and freight route from Strawberry Valley to Yreka, and many of his passengers stayed at Sisson's hostel. Sisson prospered and enlarged the hotel a little each year, adding dining rooms, bedrooms, and finally the distinctive tavern, which gave the place its reputation and name.

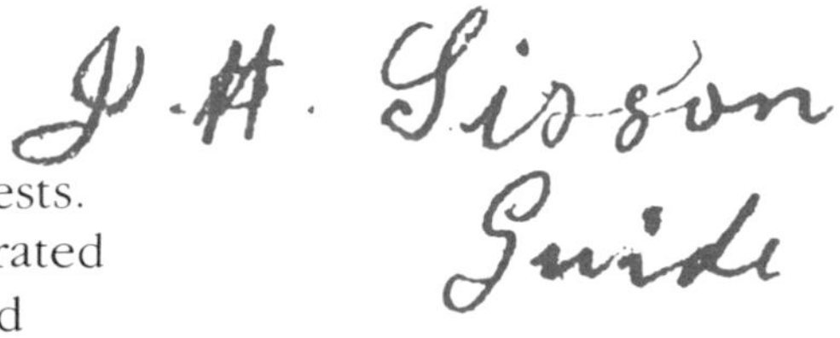

J. H. Sisson
Guide

·61·

Sisson was an urbane, educated man and kept company with intelligent, cultured people, who regarded him as a gracious host, delightful raconteur, and keen scholar of natural history. He was also considered one of the best hunters and anglers in Northern California and took as many of his guests hunting and fishing as he did mountaineering. Sisson pioneered the trail to Horse Camp and climbed Avalanche Gulch so often that the route achieved celebrity status with the American public.

Many famous American artists made the journey west to paint and sketch California's two classic scenes: Yosemite and Mt. Shasta. Painter Albert Bierstadt, who had traveled the Sierra with Clarence King, visited Sisson on several occasions with writer Fitz Hugh Ludlow, who described Sisson: "Without exception, the best rifle-shot I ever saw." John McKee, who was a member of the party that made the second ascent of Mt. Shasta, recalled that Ludlow and Bierstadt, when gazing upon one of the mountain's views, "clasped hands and tearfully rejoiced that they had lived to see that hour." Other artists, including Thomas Moran, William Keith, and Thomas Hill, regularly stayed at Sisson Tavern. Hill painted a portrait of Sisson, as well as the sign in front of the tavern, in appreciation of the hospitality he always received as a guest.

Sisson bought more land and homesteads and by the late 1870s had acquired more than six hundred acres of property where the present town of Mount Shasta is located. He also bought land along the McCloud River and built a small lodge at the river's Horseshoe Bend so his guests could enjoy the extraordinary hunting and fishing there. This land was later acquired by William Randolph Hearst, who built a lavish castle in 1903 at Sisson's favorite fishing spot.

Sisson sold most of his land to the Central Pacific Railroad Company in 1886, with an agreement that the new town be called "Sisson." He took an active role in laying out the community and even obtained five thousand Eastern Brook trout to plant in the streams flowing through the new town.

Justin Sisson's daughters entertained guests by reading tea leaves and telling fortunes.

COURTESY SISKIYOU COUNTY MUSEUM

Mt. Shasta in spring viewed from near the old Sisson Tavern across the meadows of Strawberry Valley and the town of Sisson, circa late 1890s.

EDWARD STUHL COLLECTION

One of the most interesting episodes in Sisson's life was his job transporting the U.S. Coast and Geodetic Survey's signal monument to Mt. Shasta's summit in 1875. The work could not have been done without many strong porters and packers, so Sisson employed Native American helpers. His relationship with the locals—during a time when most white settlers treated Native Americans with contempt—was a little-known facet of his life. He treated them with honesty and generosity; one of the local medicine men was so fond of Sisson that he adopted the name "Sisson Jim." It was through the natives' trust of Sisson that he was able to recruit "Sisson Jim" and others, who, in spite of superstitious fears of climbing the mountain, carried the monument tower to its summit.

When Sisson's health began to decline during the early 1890s, he spent most of his time on the grounds of the tavern, no longer able to guide mountaineers or fishers. The tavern was destroyed by fire on the evening of June 7, 1893, caused by careless handling of an oil lamp in one of the guest's rooms. Justin Sisson, who was bedridden, had to be carried from the burning building. He died at the family home on the grounds of the tavern five months later. Sisson's funeral cortege was the largest ever in Strawberry Valley, and included many of his Native American friends who had for years made his grounds, which they called "Old Sisson," their summer home. Lydia Sisson rebuilt the tavern and ran it until 1910, then sold it to a group in Yreka. The new owners continued to run the establishment, but the glamour of Sisson's hospitality and presence was gone. It was again leveled by fire, in 1916, and was never rebuilt.

The town of Sisson was officially incorporated in 1905, then the name was changed to "Mount Shasta" in 1922 by a vote of the citizens, 103 to 33. The San Francisco Chronicle called the action an "astonishing mental and moral aberration," and editorialized against the name change as an insult to the memory of Justin Sisson. "He knew more of the secrets of Mount Shasta than any living man," read the editorial of August 29, 1922. Still bearing the name of Mt. Shasta's premier guide, sportsman, and innkeeper are Sisson Elementary School, the Sisson Hatchery Museum, and Sisson Lake (the small alpine lake in the saddle between Shasta and Shastina).

·63·

Sisson Tavern, on the original stage road from Strawberry Valley to Yreka, was built in 1861 and destroyed by fire in 1893. COURTESY SIKIYOU COUNTY MUSEUM

JOHN MUIR

John Muir, perhaps the most eloquent and peripatetic naturalist the world has even known, first saw Mt. Shasta from the Sacramento River canyon during the late summer of 1874. Of that moment, he later wrote:

> When I first caught sight of it I was fifty miles away and afoot, alone and weary. Yet all my blood turned to wine, and I have not been weary since.

John Muir came to the United States as a youth from his native Scotland in 1849. After studying geology at the University of Wisconsin, he traveled to California in 1868 to study in what he referred to as "The University of the Wilderness." Muir spent the summer of 1874 in Yosemite before venturing northward for his first visit to Mt. Shasta. When he arrived at Sisson Tavern, he was unable to find anyone to join him on a climb so late in the season. Muir persuaded Sisson to outfit him with provisions and gear and, at the last minute, guide Jerome Fay agreed to take pack animals as far as the timberline with Muir's supplies. Before leaving Sisson Tavern, he wrote to his family: "Write me a line here in care of Sisson, but don't forward any letters from the Oakland office. I want only mountains until my return to civilization."

Early the next morning Muir set out for the summit with Fay accompanying him a short distance to point out the climbing route. He reached the summit at 10:30 A.M. and reveled in "the glorious landscapes spread map-like around the immense horizon, and the pathways of vanished glaciers of which Shasta had been the center." Then, despite threatening weather, Muir took time to descend to Shastina before arriving back at his timberline campsite at dusk. The following morning a storm broke, but Muir calmly occupied himself with his notebooks, magnifying lenses to observe snow crystals, and a herd of mountain sheep

John Muir, America's foremost naturalist.

COURTESY PETER PALMQUIST

•

that took shelter near his camp. The storm lasted a week, but before it was over, Sisson became worried and sent up a guide with pack animals to bring Muir back down to Strawberry Valley. During the following weeks Muir walked around the base of the mountain, visited Black Butte and Whitney Glacier, and traveled to Klamath Lake—all the while filling his notebooks with rich observations to be turned into magazine articles later.

The following year Muir was asked to return to Mt. Shasta to help with preliminary surveys and plans for the U.S. Coast and Geodetic Survey's summit monument. On April 28, 1875, John Muir, Jerome Fay, and Augustus Rodgers of the USGS climbed Mt. Shasta in good weather. Two days later, Muir and Fay made another ascent to take a series of barometric readings and reached the summit in the very rapid time of four hours, ten minutes. Their experience on Shasta's summit on April 30, 1875, is one of the most well-known events in Shasta annals, due largely to Muir's vivid descriptions.

The two planned to take barometric readings every three hours while simultaneous readings were taken by Rodgers at Sisson Tavern in Strawberry Valley, but by noon a storm began to gather and Muir decided to abandon the 3:00 P.M. observation in favor of a descent to the safety of base camp. He wrote:

> The sky speedily darkened, and just as I had completed my last observation and boxed my instruments ready for the descent, the storm began in serious earnest. After we had forced our way down the ridge and past the group of hissing fumaroles, the storm became inconceivably violent . . . . The thunder was as though the mountain were being rent to its foundations and the fires of the old volcano were breaking forth again.

Augustus Rodgers, safe at Sisson Tavern, was anxiously watching the storm clouds cover the mountain as he made entries in his diary:

> Portentious clouds cover the sky and at 2 P.M. quite a heavy thunder shower in Strawberry Valley, the clouds shutting out Shasta's peak. Hope Muir will not wait for the 3 o'clock observation of barometer.

Meanwhile, Muir and Fay decided that descent was impossible in the violence of the storm and the darkness and retreated to the hot sulphur fumaroles just below the summit pinnacle. Here they lay in the hot, steamy sludge, alternately baking on one side and freezing on the other as they turned over and over through the stormy night. Muir recalled the epic:

> The weary hours wore away like dim half-forgotten years, so long and eventful they seemed, though we did nothing but suffer . . . frozen, blistered, famished, benumbed, our bodies seemed lost to us at times. "Are you suffering much?" Jerome would inquire with pitiful faintness. "Yes," I would say, striving to keep my voice brave, "frozen and burned; but never mind, Jerome, the night will wear away at last, and tomorrow we go a-Maying, and what campfires we will make, and what sun-baths we will take!"

By morning the storm had subsided, but the summit plateau was bitterly cold. Muir and Fay made their way slowly through snow drifts, scarcely able to bend their frozen trousers.

·65·

Sheep Rock. John Muir visited this area, finding caves and horns from wild sheep, when he walked around the mountain in 1874.

1870 Carleton Watkins photograph. COURTESY USGS

When they reached the Red Banks, the sun began to warm them and they were able to descend more rapidly. The pair reached their basecamp at 10:00 A.M. and half an hour later were pleasantly surprised to hear Sisson shouting for them in the forest.

Augustus Rodgers remembered the sight of the two returning to the tavern:

> Muir and Fay both look as if they had been on a "terrible tear"—eyes bloodshot, faces red and swollen and altogether two very disreputable looking persons. Mr. Muir regretted that he could not answer my inquiry as to the degree of cold by saying that while his back was scalding, his beard and watch chain and two barometer guards were all frozen together.

Muir was given an "awful dose of coffee and whiskey" by Sisson and put to bed. The next morning, Muir recalled, "Sisson's children came in with flowers and covered my bed, and the storm on the mountain top vanished like a dream."

Muir never climbed Mt. Shasta again, but he returned to the area nearly a dozen more times. In the fall of 1877 he led a botanical excursion on Shasta's lower slopes with Asa Gray and Sir Joseph Hooker, two of the most famous botanists in the world at that time. In 1888 he came to Shasta with his good friend and fellow Scot, artist William Keith, to gather material for the magazine *Picturesque California* and to visit the ailing Sisson.

"On the Big Bend." Drawing by William Fitler for "Picturesque California," which John Muir edited.

Original summit register entries from John Muir's two climbs for preliminary surveys for the Coast and Geodetic Survey's summit monument. The second entry, April 30, 1875, preceded Muir and Jerome Fay's epic overnight at the summit during a terrible storm. COURTESY BANCROFT LIBRARY

Muir later toured the world and worked tirelessly for the establishment of national parks and recreation areas. His writings compelled a young nation that was rapidly destroying its wild heritage to preserve scenic wildlands for the enrichment of its future generations. "I care to live only to entice people to look at nature," he wrote. John Muir's notes, books, and other writings on Mt. Shasta reveal his love for the mountain that for him was "the pole-star of the landscape."

JOAQUIN MILLER

"Lonely as God, and white as a winter moon, Mount Shasta starts up sudden and solitary from the heart of the great black forests of Northern California." These words from *Life Amongst the Modocs,* written by author Joaquin Miller in 1873, have endured as one of the most famous descriptions of Mt. Shasta.

Miller, one of the most colorful and complex characters in Mt. Shasta's history, came to the area as a teenager from Oregon. He only lived there from 1854 to 1857, yet this period of his life was the most significant in shaping his literary career. Miller used his experiences in the Shasta area as the basis for scores of books, poems, and plays, all of which made him one of the most famous writers in late nineteenth-century Europe and America. Miller worked at gold mines near Yreka and Castle Crags and lived for nearly a year with the Wintun and Shasta tribes south of McCloud. He married a Native American, and they named their daughter Cali-Shasta. Then, in late 1857, Miller abruptly left Mt. Shasta, becoming a pony express agent, a surveyor, and even a judge in various western states before he began to write.

Miller's real name was Cincinnatus Hiner Miller. He adopted the name Joaquin after the famous Mexican bandit Joaquin Murietta, who was popularized as the Mexican Robin Hood during the 1850s. The idea came from Miller's friend and fellow writer, Ina Coolbrith, who thought the colorful name would help Miller's career as a writer.

·67·

Joaquin Miller, "The poet of the Sierras," in 1899.

Miller's writings did much to envelop Mt. Shasta in an aura of romance

and mystery that has endured to this day.

COURTESY MERIAM LIBRARY

William Simpson's sketch for the London Illustrated News when the Modoc Wars were international news. Joaquin Miller exaggerated his own experiences during the war and his Life Amongst the Modocs *became a bestseller in Europe. (William Simpson was the same newspaper artist whose sketch of the Crimea War inspired Tennyson's "Charge of the Light Brigade.")*

Miller freely interchanged fact and fancy in his writing. He was wont to take the leading events of Northern California history, insert himself as the central figure in them, and change the facts to suit him. His reasons for taking such broad artistic license were never completely understood by his critics. On one level were fame, book sales, and an adoring readership; but on another level he was inspired with feelings for nature, the land, and the people who lived there. Miller justified his literary exaggerations by citing his compassion for Native Americans:

> I must write of myself, because I was among these people of whom I write . . . a silent and mysterious people, a race of prophets; poets without the gift of expression—a race that has been mistreated, and never understood—a race that is moving noiselessly from the face of the earth.

He became an impassioned spokesperson for Native Americans at a time when it was unpopular to advocate their rights and wrote environmental manifestoes after seeing what reckless mining was doing to the land. His works were important descriptions of what the land and natives were like just as white settlers began to affect them.

When Miller lived at Castle Crags, he fought in a battle with the Wintun or Shasta tribe that was precipitated when miners angered them by ruining the salmon fishery with silt and mine tailings. Miller later referred to these miners as "madmen." He was wounded during the fight, reportedly the last battle in California where the natives used only bows and arrows. In Miller's later book, *Life Amongst the Modocs,* the story was embellished: the Shasta and the Wintun became the dreaded Modocs, and the battle took on epic proportions.

Miller went to London in 1870, then again in 1873, shortly after the famous Modoc wars broke out in northeast California. His book became an overnight bestseller to a European audience that cared little if "Modoc" was substituted for "Wintun,"

or "Sierra" for "Shasta." Miller, the self-proclaimed "Poet of the Sierras," insinuated himself into the highest British literary circles, where his admirers were charmed by his long hair and western dress. The *London Examiner* said of Miller's book:

> As interesting as a novel and picturesque as a poem, it is an eloquent and most timely apology for the unfortunate people whom the progress of American "civilization" is rapidly exterminating.

Mark Twain attended literary gatherings with Miller in London and recommended *Life Amongst the Modocs* to his American publisher. Walt Whitman and Robert Browning also admired Miller's work, but Bret Harte, also a champion of Native American rights, claimed that nothing Miller wrote was true. The American press, not as lenient with Miller's factual contretemps as the Europeans, refused to review the book. The gloss of Miller's initial literary achievements finally faded under criticism, but he continued to write for a loyal, if not smaller audience. His play "Danites in the Sierras," which was set near the Yreka gold mines, was performed on Broadway and in London.

Discharge papers from the real Modoc War. Joaquin Miller used his experiences during a minor skirmish at Castle Crags to claim participation in the Modoc War. COURTESY CHRIS SCHNEIDER COLLECTION

Miller claimed to have climbed Mt. Shasta in the year variously given by himself in different writings as 1854 and 1856. The story of his climb as told in *Life Amongst the Modocs* was exciting, humorous, and unique and probably thrilled his reading audience. There was, however, a strong feeling of contrivance to the whole tale, and nothing showed that Miller had even a hint of knowledge of the climbing route on the mountain. According to Miller, he had been working as a guide for "Mountain Joe" in Castle Crags and had been entrusted to guide the very first party up Mt. Shasta, a group of "travelling, solemn, self-important-looking missionaries in black clothes, spectacles, and beaver hats." Miller related how the missionaries had failed to be impressed by the glory of nature on all sides, caring only to recite prayers on the summit; how he found them to be the "most sour, selfish and ungrateful wretches on earth;" and how they paid him for leading them to the summit with prayers and sermons. The memory of the climb was so distasteful, according to Miller, that he never wanted to repeat the experience.

In 1892 Miller confessed that *Life Amongst the Modocs* had been hastily written while he was living in London in 1873, when accounts of the Modoc War had reached Europe and the demand for books and stories about the war was great. Miller let it be known that he had lived among the Modocs, and so "in great haste, and with a confusion of fact and fiction, a volume was brought out by the Queen's publisher." Miller said, in referring to himself, that "the author expected this book to quietly die when it had done its work; but, as it seems determined to outlive him, with all its follies and fictions, he has taken it severely in hand, cut off all its fictitious growth, and confined its leaves to the cold, frozen truth." When the 1892 rewrite, *My Life Among the Indians,* appeared, many previous exaggerations, as well as the story of Miller's ascent of Mt. Shasta with the missionaries, was conspicuously missing.

Whether his works were, indeed, fact or fiction, Miller was an excellent writer. He wrote several articles for Muir's *Picturesque California* travel magazine that were ecological treatises in their descriptions of local wildlife and habitat and subtle reminders to consider the harmony and balance of nature in the Shasta area. His "Game Regions of the Upper Sacramento" is still considered a classic of outdoor writing:

> Were I asked to put a finger on the one most favored spot to be found on the map of the world for rod and gun and restful camp, I would indicate the tributary waters of the Sacramento, with Mount Shasta for a tent.

Miller continued to write until his death in 1913. Many critics considered him eccentric, but he held fast to advocacy of Native Americans and the land, even if fact and imagination became intertwined in his writings. Miller remained rooted strongly to his Mt. Shasta experiences with a feeling for place that remained for him a constant theme:

> Mount Shasta was before me. For the first time I now looked upon the mountain in whose shadows so many tragedies were to be enacted; the most comely and perfect snow peak in America.

THE SIERRA CLUB CABIN AND MAC OLBERMAN

M. Hall McAllister was a prominent San Francisco judge, and an early Sierra Club member and outdoorsman. During the early part of the century, he hosted a touring group of Japanese mountaineers who wanted to visit Mt. Shasta after hearing of its resemblance to Mt. Fuji. He took them to the popular timberline base camp at Horse Camp, whereupon they expressed surprise that there was no hut or cabin. After all, Mt. Fuji had a series of huts nearly to its summit, and in the European Alps huts and refuges were everywhere. The seeds were planted, and, largely

The Sierra Club's Shasta Alpine Lodge, built in 1922

through McAllister's effort and generosity, the Sierra Club's Shasta Alpine Lodge came to exist.

The club purchased land surrounding Horse Camp and began construction in July 1922. Two stonemasons, two carpenters, two laborers, and a cook—with occasional help from other craftspeople—used predominately native materials in constructing the large one-room building. Rocks were gathered and squared off with stone chisels. If the rocks were too far away or too large, they were skidded down to the building site on a rough sled behind horses. Tailings and chips from the cut stones still remain near the fire circle in front of the cabin. The roof beams and rafters were hewn from Shasta red fir timber, and they, too, remain today in their original state. A corrugated metal roof was installed, which also remains, and the finishing touches were completed in the early summer of 1923. When Shasta Alpine Lodge was dedicated on July 4, 1923, the Wintun tribe gave McAllister the honorary name, "Yola Wintu," meaning "snow man," or "man who builds a house in the snow."

"Mac" Olberman on Shasta's summit after a five-hour ascent just before his 70th birthday in 1932.

"Mac" with his steel crowbar, returning from work on the causeway. EDWARD STUHL COLLECTION

McAllister bore the costs of cabin upkeep and maintenance and sent frequent packages of food, ginger ale, and other treats to the summer custodian. He was also responsible for the decorative wrought-iron silhouettes that stand atop four stone columns around the lodge and even had a selection of high-altitude flora shipped from the Himalayas and planted in the front courtyard area.

J. M. "Mac" Olberman, one of the laborers who helped with the lodge's construction, was retained by McAllister as the first custodian. Mac's early personal history is obscure. Evidently he had come west from his native Kentucky to work on the railroad, then drifted and held odd jobs. All the while he read and educated himself to a remarkably high standard. He taught himself German and Norwegian, and one of the classic published translations of Ibsen's "Brand" is Mac's work. A rumor persisted that his education came while serving a jail term for a wrongly accused murder, but even his close friend, mountaineer Edward Stuhl, was never sure of this.

Mac's great love was Mt. Shasta, and he expressed it through his position as lodge custodian. Over his twelve-year tenure he served innumerable meals to hungry climbers, built several wood cabins and shelters, constructed an elaborate kitchen, and never failed to leave a lantern or candle in the window of the cabin to serve as a beacon for any climbers caught by darkness. When Mac was sixty-six he climbed to the summit with a gentleman of sixty-eight in five hours, seventeen minutes. "He was the first person I ever accompanied to the summit who did not delay me by resting or loitering on the way," Mac recalled of his companion. On another climb Mac and Stuhl carried a surveyor's chain, measuring the distance to the summit and erecting stone cairns at each mile. The two once made a nonstop climb to the summit in the impressive time of five hours. Stuhl remembered Mac refusing to take a break or rest, while reciting the poetry of Byron without repeating a verse the whole way. This climb took place on the eve of Mac's seventieth birthday!

Mac's greatest project was the construction of his Causeway. This trail, made of huge flat stones, ascends nearly a mile up the mountain and is of immeasurable benefit to climbers starting out in early morning or returning, tired and hungry, after dark. Past sixty when he began, Mac worked nine years on the Causeway; some of the stones he moved probably weigh more than one thousand pounds, yet he worked alone. Stuhl once recalled how Mac, "a scarecrow incarnate," would only chuckle when asked how he moved such large stones. His heavy, steel crowbar—six feet long—still resides in the lodge, and visitors may heft its bulk and imagine what it must have been like to build Mac Olberman's Causeway.

RECORD ASCENTS AND THE 1925 MARATHON

As long as people have climbed mountains, unofficial records and rivalries have developed. John Muir probably held the first record for the fastest ascent of Mt. Shasta, with a time of four hours, ten minutes in 1875. Considering that today's average climber takes between six and nine hours to scale the mountain, Muir's time was excellent. Muir's record stood for eight years. In 1883, Harry Babcock of San Francisco was credited by witnesses with making the climb from Horse Camp to the summit in three hours, forty-five minutes. His time remained unchallenged for forty years.

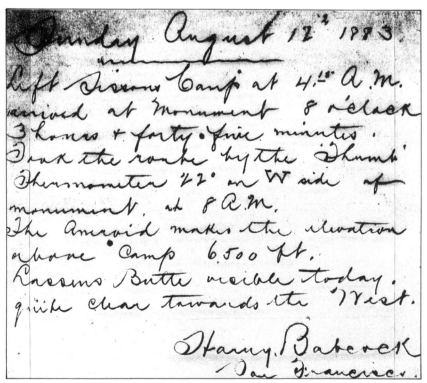

Summit register entry for Harry Babcock's 1883 claimed record ascent.

Mt. Shasta Marathon

Race Starts at 9:30 A. M. Sunday Morning, July 5, 1925, from the Lodge.

Entrance Fee (none)—Entries Close Morning of Race

Sierra Club Pack Train will leave Trail Bridge at 3:00 P. M., July 4th, to carry blankets and outfits of hikers to Lodge.

Prizes—First: Cash, $50; J. H. Sisson Memorial Cup, pure silver, value $50.00; hiking boots, value $15.00.

Second Prize: $15.00 and Alpine Ice Axe.

Third Prize: $10.00 and Pair Skiis and Ski Sticks.

All accident liability for individual account.

Judges and Starters: Jesse R. Hall, J. W. Schuler.

Judges: Roy Carter, J. M. Olberman.

Autos may be taken to three-mile post.
Coffee and Bread Free—Hikers to furnish blankets and food.

In 1923 Norman Clyde was teaching high school in nearby Weaverville. Clyde had already established himself as one of America's foremost mountaineers by making numerous first ascents of many of the Sierra Nevada's major peaks. On July 3, 1923, he made the climb from Horse Camp to the summit in three hours, seventeen minutes. After resting a day, Clyde cut the time to a remarkable two hours, forty-three minutes. There were four witnesses present, and the time was certified by Mac Olberman, the custodian of the Sierra Club Lodge. Newspapers dutifully reported, "Norman Clyde now holds the undisputed record for climbing Mt. Shasta," and the feat was made "official" by the approval of the Sierra Club of San Francisco. Clyde's time was extraordinary, but in only six weeks Barney McCoy, a guide and rancher in Gazelle, just north of Mt. Shasta, claimed a faster time—an incredible two hours, seventeen minutes. However, McCoy had no witnesses. Controversy prevailed and the Sierra Club Lodge Committee, the unofficial sanctioning body for Shasta's record times, refused to recognize the claim. McCoy was invited to try the climb again before witnesses, and the Sierra Club offered to put up a prize for a record time. Thus was born the Mount Shasta Marathon.

The Mt. Shasta Chamber of Commerce and the Sierra Club enthusiastically decided to sponsor an annual race to the summit of Mt. Shasta to coincide with local Fourth of July celebrations. Prizes and cash were offered, including the J. H. Sisson Memorial Cup. This beautiful silver trophy was donated by none other than Harry Babcock, the record holder in 1883. When race day arrived on July 5, only seven contestants had registered; it was considered a foregone conclusion that Barney McCoy would win regardless of the competition, and this, no doubt, had frightened off other competitors. However, an unheralded eighteen-year-old logging camp helper, David Lawyer, surprised everyone by winning easily in the outstanding time of two hours, twenty-four minutes. He had arrived in town the previous week and climbed the mountain the day before the contest to familiarize himself with the route!

The original announcement for the 1925 Mt. Shasta Marathon.

The contest was a dramatic event. The summit judges, led by Mac Olberman, left early, taking a separate route so the contestants would have to break their own trail. As the climbers left Horse Camp, Barney McCoy immediately took the lead. David Lawyer started in light tennis shoes and soon drifted off-route as he tried to avoid the snowfields by leaping from rock to rock. He soon realized his mistake, changed into the heavier boots he was carrying, and chased after the other contestants. McCoy was far ahead, but breaking trail in the soft snow took its toll and he was forced to stop and rest at the Red Banks. Lawyer passed McCoy while he was resting and reached the summit ahead of him. McCoy arrived thirteen minutes later. Lawyer never climbed Mt. Shasta again, and the marathon was discontinued after its singular appearance. An attempt was made to reinstate the event at the Mt. Shasta Ski Bowl in 1960, but this, too, was short-lived.

Many other excellent climbs have been made since the 1925 Marathon, but lack of notoriety and "unofficial" conditions have failed to rekindle the excitement present in 1925. On June 22, 1985, Robert Webb, then custodian of the Sierra Club Lodge, climbed from the cabin to the summit in one hour, forty-seven minutes. Several witnesses with synchronized watches verified the feat. On July 5, 1985, Webb, superbly fit from summers at the cabin, broke his own record with a time of one hour, thirty-nine minutes. It was fitting that the date the new record was set was on the sixtieth anniversary of the original Mt. Shasta Marathon.

Upper left: The seven Marathon contestants, faces blackened for protection against the sun. Eventual winner, David Lawyer, is at the left. Barney McCoy, the previous record-holder is 3rd from right.

EDWARD STUHL COLLECTION

Left: David Lawyer, winner of the 1925 summit marathon.

EDWARD STUHL COLLECTION

Right: Robert Webb, current custodian of the Shasta Alpine Lodge, and record-holder of the fastest climb: 1 hour 39 minutes. Webb is holding the crowbar "Mac" Olberman used to move rocks for "Olberman's Causeway."

EDWARD STUHL

In June 1917, Edward Stuhl walked up the same Sacramento River canyon that John Muir had traveled forty years earlier. Stuhl's great love was painting and photographing mountain wildflowers, and his pack was filled with paints, easels, and cameras, as well as camping gear. Three years earlier, botanizing and painting Central Valley wildflowers, he saw Mt. Lassen's eruption and had recorded the spectacular event on film and in his diary. When Stuhl reached the area in the river canyon near Dunsmuir where John Muir first sighted Mt. Shasta, he was equally overcome. His journal entry for June 30, 1917, read:

> I was surprised by one of the grandest sights I have ever beheld. An unforgettable picture to the last moment of one's life. There it rose above the canyon framed by dark forest-clad hillsides, bathed in sunlight. Was it a mirage or a fantastic upbuilding of rose-tinted, silver-edged, blue-shaded clouds? A vision suspended in mid air. I doubted its reality, but it was truly Mt. Shasta. I had not seen a real mountain for many years. And such a mountain with eternal snow and probably glacier ice on. Of such height and dimensions, majesty and beauty, it makes faint any attempt to describe it. These are impressions to settle deep. And here I sit in California at the foot and in the spell of Shasta. Old Dreams and new longings arise, the love for the mountains of a stray mountaineer; the restless impulse for adventure and conquest . . . and conquer I will this mountain.

Stuhl was born in 1887 in Budapest, Hungary, and raised near the southern Austrian town of Graz. His father owned a large stained-glass studio, and Stuhl apprenticed in the craft at

Edward Stuhl at Shasta's summit, September, 1931.

·75·

an early age and attended the Academy of Art in Munich. Stuhl often spent his summers traveling throughout the Bavarian countryside to repair church windows that had suffered winter storm damage. During these summers he walked to Vienna and Salzburg, through the Tirol mountains, and along the entire Adriatic coast of Yugoslavia.

Many years later he recalled that a turning point in his life occurred when he saw the original Wild Bill Hickok and Annie Oakley "Wild West Show" in Munich. The event, coupled with his appetite for James Fennimore Cooper, Mark Twain, and other American frontier authors, kindled a thirst to see "real cowboys and Indians" and the American West. In 1908 his father arranged for him to work in a large stained-glass studio in Chicago, and Stuhl, with his new wife Rosie, was soon on his way to America. But it was only a few years before the couple became restless with city life. Some old European friends living in Mexico wrote them exciting letters about Central America, and when the friends offered to turn over the management of a large ranch to the Stuhls, they left Chicago for Mexico at once.

The cattle ranch, nearly a quarter-million acres, was a three-day ride from the nearest town and post office. When the Mexican Revolution broke out, the Stuhls were befriended by none other than Pancho Villa. After the tumultuous times of the revolution quieted, they decided to return to Europe, but not before first visiting the 1915 Panama-Pacific International Exposition in San Francisco. Their return to Austria was then indefinitely postponed while World War I ravaged Europe, so they spent several years exploring Northern California, painting mountain wildflowers, and managing Central Valley duck hunting clubs for well-heeled San Francisco sportsmen. When one duck club member, Charles Wheeler of San Francisco, invited the Stuhls to his ranch on the McCloud River just south of Mt. Shasta, a very long and permanent association with the mountain began.

Edward Stuhl skiing at age 76.

Edward Stuhl heating water for tea in the summit hot springs.

"It was cold enough that I had to wear heavy gloves in the process."

Shasta Lily from Edward Stuhl's collection of watercolor

paintings of Mt. Shasta's wildflowers.

COURTESY MERIAM LIBRARY

From 1923 to 1946 the Stuhls worked for William Randolph Hearst at the publisher's famous Wintun estate along the McCloud River. In the late 1920s, Stuhl nearly convinced Hearst to purchase Southern Pacific Railroad land on Mt. Shasta—at $2 an acre—for donation to the state of California for a park. The state had already agreed to pay half, but Hearst was occupied with other interests and the opportunity was lost.

The Stuhls later settled in a log cabin west of the town of Mount Shasta and lived an active life until well into their nineties. They both skied until their eighties, and Ed, who climbed every major mountain in western North America from Mexico to Canada, made a solo winter climb of Mexico's 17,887-foot Popocatepetl when he was seventy-six.

Ed Stuhl's knowledge of Mt. Shasta's history, and his skill as a raconteur, delighted for years the many climbers and hikers who met him on the mountain. He rarely missed a weekend at the Sierra Club's Shasta Alpine Lodge, and his recall was astounding, such that he could accurately relate details in building the lodge, epics of his early winter climbs, tales about the lodge's first custodian, Mac Olberman, or exactly where he had gone to find and paint a particular wildflower. During the weeks of the first soft-landing on Mars, Ed was fond of telling his young audiences about his astonishment and disbelief at hearing the news of an earlier historic event: the Wright brothers' first flight.

Ed Stuhl's great hope was to live long enough to see Mt. Shasta preserved as a national or state park, or wilderness area, and he worked tirelessley to protect it. He was saddened, but stoic, during each Congressional failure to pass protective legislation for the mountain. Ed died February 15, 1984, only a few months before the Mt. Shasta Wilderness Area was designated by Congress. A legacy, however, remains: a published collection of his paintings of Mt. Shasta's wildflowers, and the love and appreciation for the mountain that he instilled in everyone he met.

·77·

Huge pine logs on McCloud River Railroad flatcar, early 1900s.

COURTESY SISKIYOU COUNTY MUSEUM

CHAPTER 6

LOGGING, LUMBER, AND RAILROADS

WILLIAM WIGGINS CAME TO MT. SHASTA IN 1840 AFTER TAKING A CLIPPER SHIP AROUND SOUTH AMERICA AND LANDING AT THE RUSSIAN SETTLEMENT OF FORT ROSS ABOVE SAN FRANCISCO. When he returned to visit friends and relatives in his native St. Louis in 1847, they plied him with all sorts of questions about California. He recalled:

> People were always quizzing me as to the truth of the information they had received in regard to matters in California. A bystander said he had heard that the timber was so tall that a gun was not necessary in hunting squirrels—you had only to scare one up those tall trees, and when he got nigh the top, his head would swim from lack of air, and he would come tumbling!

Such were the tales of Northern California's woods.

"Logging with ox-teams in the Shasta Region," from John Muir's "Picturesque California."

·79·

Logging was one of the first industries in the homesteads and townships surrounding Mt. Shasta, and to the early settlers at the foot of the mountain, the tall evergreen forests must have seemed limitless. Siskiyou County has always been home to a rich assortment of trees; Russian Peak, 35 miles west of Mt. Shasta, is considered by many botanists and silviculturists to be the location of one of the most diverse coniferous forests in the world. A great variety of trees, including many commercially desirable species, grows on Mt. Shasta's slopes, including Ponderosa, Jeffrey, and sugar pine; Douglas, white, and Shasta red fir; incense cedar; and hemlock.

During the early part of the twentieth century, the famous American architects Henry and Charles Greene specified straight-grained fir and Port Orford cedar from Siskiyou County for their trend-setting "California bungalow" style homes.

Horse logging in 1895 near the present town of Mount Shasta.

COURTESY U. S. FOREST SERVICE

Logging with oxen in the Sacramento Canyon in the 1890s.

"Big wheels" logging in the late 1890s—early 1900s.

Violin maker Louis Bedell found that the wood from the Shasta red fir made excellent violins and violas—comparable to the fine spruce instruments made by Europe's best luthiers. During the early 1930s he made Amati and Stradivarius reproductions that were coveted by violinists worldwide.

Prior to the building of the railroads, lumber was only cut in the Mt. Shasta area for local use: homes, barns, mining sluice boxes and flumes, and bridges. Early sawmills at first used hand-operated pit saws, then simple water-powered mechanisms to saw the lumber. They got the logs from homestead lands or helped themselves to public domain "Government timber." At this time the Forest Service had not yet come into existence and public lands were not carefully managed. A good water-powered sawmill could cut five to fifteen hundred feet of lumber per day, based upon the water available. Boards were sold right at the mill, and $10 per thousand feet of lumber was considered a fair price.

Frank Nicols owned a small mill near Mt. Shasta in the 1880s.

It didn't cost much to make lumber in those days, since I cut free Government timber, then hired a man and a team to haul in the logs. I ran the mill by myself, so I didn't have any payroll to meet, and the only supply bill was for axle grease for the saw.

Before the turn of the century loggers used teams of oxen or horses to drag logs out of the forest and as far as 3 or 4 miles to the sawmill. A woodsman rounded off, or "sniped" the ends of the logs so they would drag easier, but at best this kind of logging was very slow and difficult. Wagons using cut logs for wheels were used for bigger loads and greater distances. Stronger, more dependable wagon wheels were also made, with steel rims using wooden wedges to maintain a tight fit, but these rough conveyances could not carry large loads and were limited to gentle terrain. Later, an advancement in timber trans-

·81·

portation came with the "big wheels," a strong yoke with ten- to twelve-foot wheels that could cradle large logs beneath the axle.

The first significant breakthrough in logging efficiency was the use of portable steam-powered machinery to haul timber out of the forest, often over terrain that was too steep and rugged for draft animals. Early models of the Dolbeer

"Steam Donkey," invented in 1882 at Eureka, California, were used in Siskiyou County, where they gained immediate acceptance by the growing timber industry. The Best Company, predecessor of the Caterpillar Tractor Company in the San Francisco Bay Area, manufactured steam "traction engines" (later called simply "tractors"), the prototypes of which were first used in the forests surrounding Mt. Shasta.

·82·

The Best Company's "steam traction engine" in use near Mt. Shasta in 1895.

COURTESY U. S. FOREST SERVICE

THE RAILROAD

After Lieutenant George Emmons and his small overland party from the Wilkes Expedition descended the steep Sacramento River Canyon from Mt. Shasta to the plains during the autumn of 1841, they unequivocally recommended against construction of a railroad along the route. During the 1850s the Pacific Railroad Surveys nevertheless considered the canyon, in addition to several other potential routes from California to Oregon on both sides of the Cascades. Lieutenant Robert Williamson led one survey party through the Sacramento Canyon to the Columbia River in 1855, along the way estimating the height of Mt. Shasta at 18,000 feet.

The Railway Acts of the early 1860s were the deciding motivation needed for the Central Pacific Railroad to seriously consider a California-Oregon rail line. The federal government provided land, low-interest loans to contractors, and military protection from potentially hostile Native Americans. The railroads took the financial risks, usually borrowing capital against their newly acquired lands, and, if successful, reaped the commercial benefits from exploiting new territory and markets. As early as 1850 Congress had already granted nearly seven million public domain acres to such projects.

A railroad route through the steep Sacramento River Canyon and over the rugged Siskiyou Mountains on the California-Oregon border was eventually decided upon. More than two thousand people, mostly Chinese laborers, worked on the difficult section through the Sacramento Canyon, and the track finally reached Strawberry Valley at the foot of Mt. Shasta by December 1886. Contractors and civil engineers agreed that it was one of the most difficult railroad grades they had ever built.

The resulting railroad service between Portland and San Francisco was called the Shasta Route, and was described as the "Road of a Thousand Wonders" in the railroad's advertising. The line became a popular tourist attraction as well as an important commercial artery, providing connections with Central Pacific's transcontinental routes.

The railroad and logging went hand in hand in Siskiyou County. The new rail lines opened thousands of acres of timberland and permitted marketing and sales of lumber and wood products in distant markets like Sacramento, San Francisco, and Los Angeles. Settlements sprang up throughout the Sacramento Canyon and Strawberry Valley, and by the beginning of the twentieth century there were more than one hundred sawmills along the Sacramento River from Mt. Shasta to today's Shasta Lake, many with colorful names like Rainbow, Mott, and Azalea. Several of the smaller mills provided lumber and cordwood to the railroad, which required more then thirty million board-feet a year for ties, bridges, fuel, and protective snowsheds.

"The Shasta Route, Road of a Thousand Wonders." California-Oregon express train #16 near Edgewood in the early 1900s.

COURTESY SISKIYOU COUNTY MUSEUM

·83·

Skills like blacksmithing, saw filing, steamfitting, and machine work were in high demand and attracted many new settlers to the Mt. Shasta area. Immigrants became an important segment of the labor force: Swedes from the Scandinavian forests, Italians from the Dolomite mountains, and African-Americans from the pine-producing regions of Alabama and Georgia, already experienced in lumbering, all came to Mt. Shasta. Chinese, Japanese, Irish, Greeks, and Latinos played a major role in constructing the main railroad lines and the hundreds of miles of spur lines that followed. Many second and third generation relatives of those early settlers remain in Siskiyou County, accounting for the cultural diversity of the area.

When timber production peaked in the first half of the twentieth century, the large mills in Weed, McCloud, and Mount Shasta were producing more than two million board-feet of lumber per day in their combined operations. The smaller mills were eventually replaced by large, highly mechanized operations that utilized railroad transportation, overhead cable systems, and flumes many miles long to bring timber out of the mountains. Spurs, or secondary track lines extended into the surrounding territory to access new stands of trees and in certain areas of nearby Shasta County to bring minerals and ore to smelters. By 1910 more than 200 miles of spur track had been laid, and by the middle of the century the large mills in McCloud and Weed had built, relocated, and removed more than 2,000 miles of track. The "Weed Logger" left the town of Weed early each morning, making stops at Grass Lake, Leaf, Murphy, Yannah, Mt. Hebron, and all the logging camps north and east of the mountain to pick up log-laden flatcars for the sawmills.

Railroad logging was not without its problems, including the common California tortoiseshell butterfly. This butterfly multiplies in enormous numbers on Shasta's slopes during spring and summer, and during 1914 so many of the larvae congregated on the spur tracks used for logging that they made them too slippery for the heavy trains to begin moving, once stopped, or braked to a stop, once moving. A clever McCloud River Railroad mechanic solved the problem by using jets of steam from the locomotive to clear the insects from the track, and his ingenious method was featured in the popular magazine, *Scientific American*.

Other railroad spurs and sidings were built to collect water from the abundant mineral springs in the Sacramento River Canyon. The Castle Rock, Shasta Springs, and Ney Springs water companies shipped bottled water, as well as bulk liquid, in special tin-lined tank cars throughout the West to a thirsty public convinced of the curative and health benefits of Mt. Shasta water.

In 1929 the Great Depression put many mills out of business. Those that survived found the old railroad logging too expensive and much slower than the new gasoline- and diesel-powered logging trucks that could make two or three trips a day. Also, the move from large tracts of easily accessible company lands to steeper terrain and smaller blocks of Forest Service lands made rail logging uneconomical. Today, almost all of the many hundreds of miles of logging spur tracks and sidings that were built in the early days have been removed. The rail beds remain on Mt. Shasta's north and east sides, mostly overgrown with second-growth fir and pine, but still yielding occasional track spikes to the sharp eyes of railroad buffs.

PEAK PRODUCTION

Of all the trees surrounding Mt. Shasta during the first half of this century, pine was the most prolific and was logged the most extensively. James Nile, retired chief forester for Southern Pacific Land Company's Shasta operations recalled that he knew of no large inland California area with better terrain for the commercial harvest of pine than the lands extending from Mt. Shasta's eastern base, commonly called the McCloud Flats. Millions of board-feet of pine were annually cut in the forests surrounding the mountain and shipped by railroad to industries that favored the clear, strong wood for doors, windows, furniture, decorative moldings, and "box shook," the sawn wooden parts for fruit and vegetable crates. Metal foundries and toolmakers also preferred pine for pattern stock because it was easily worked and held its shape.

During the 1915 Panama-Pacific International Exposition in San Francisco, held to inaugurate the Panama Canal's opening, the Weed and McCloud River lumber companies joined forces with the Red River Lumber Company in Westwood, California—100 miles southeast of Mt. Shasta—to sponsor a

promotional display. The Red River Lumber Company, owned by the Great Lakes timber baron, T. B. Walker, was one of the largest lumber companies in the United States and, together with the Weed and McCloud mills, cut a prodigious amount of pine. They constructed a hall called The White and Sugar Pine Building, to exhibit their wood products and attract new customers. The structure was made almost entirely of local woods, including liberal amounts of attractive pine trim, and featured fireplaces made of lava rock from Mt. Shasta's slopes.

When lumber production reached record volumes in the 1920s, the mills surrounding Mt. Shasta had such an abundance of premium pine wood that it became economical to ship lumber and wood products to the East Coast. Many enterprising Northern California mill owners advertised their ponderosa pine wood, technically a yellow pine, as "California white pine," and shipped it East to compete with mills producing eastern white pine, a wood highly desirable for fancy trim and finish work that brought a premium price. The eastern mills objected to the competition and accused the western mills of fraud and false advertising, asserting that their wood was the real white pine and that the other was only its inferior yellow cousin at best.

Several years of rancorous accusations, countercharges, and threats of court action followed between the East and West Coast mills. Finally, the Federal Trade Commission correctly concluded that the ponderosa was *not*, in fact, white pine, and enjoined the Northern California mills—including the Weed, Siskiyou, McCloud, and Cantara mills, among many others, from using such phrases as "the celebrated California white pine lumber" and "California white pine is the real stuff!" in their advertising.

·85·

Abner Weed Railroad #1, the "Weed Logger," bringing lumber

to the mills from logging camp spur lines, 1902.

COURTESY SISKIYOU COUNTY MUSEUM

TRANSITION AND DECLINE OF THE LUMBER INDUSTRY

The U.S. Forest Service began to sell timber from the Shasta Forest Reserves in the early teens, soon after the agency came into existence under President Theodore Roosevelt. Large-scale Forest Service timber sales began in the 1940s, coinciding with the depletion of the best private timberlands, the post-World War II housing boom, and a growing market for other species of trees that developed as pine became less abundant. The mills surrounding Mt. Shasta began to diversify their operations to remain economically viable, cutting different woods and manufacturing plywood and chip stock. Douglas fir was structurally strong and suitable for the construction trades; incense cedar's weather-resistant properties made it desirable for roofing shakes, shingles, and wood-clad pencils; Port Orford cedar was exported to Japan where it was valued for its resemblance to Hinoki, a wood the Japanese treasure in home and temple construction.

Mt. Shasta's surrounding forests have been subject to the peak and decline of the timber industry, the reduction of old growth, and larger conservation issues. Many private mills fell victim to boom-and-bust economic cycles and overcut their private timberlands before the middle of the twentieth century. Surprisingly, many large private landowners and companies sold their land and timber outright, not establishing their own timber management programs until the 1940s and 1950s. The result was a rapid decline in large, prolific old-growth forests. Foresters, and forestry as a science, had little authority to influence management decisions, and concepts like sustained yield and long cutting rotations to insure maximum growth of timber were ignored in favor of quick profits.

The U.S.—indeed, even the world's—timber industry has historically been sensitive to the winds of change and strongly affected by economic trends, resource availability, and, more recently, corporate decisions. Recent years have seen large-scale ownership consolidations, sales, trades, leveraged buy-outs, and the rapid liquidation of timber on western forest lands to satisfy stockholders—manipulations that wreak havoc on a resource-based economy and good forest management. The result is that forest management, land-use planning, and resource conservation are now objects of global public concern.

"The spirit of this tonic mineral water stirs all other liquids into life and joins them in one mellow beverage."

Mineral springs near the railroad at north Dunsmuir.

The Upton lumber mill during the early 1900s heydey of lumber production. Black Butte in background.

·86·

Today, most of the mills surrounding Mt. Shasta have closed. The town of Mount Shasta's last operating mill, P & M Lumber Company, closed in 1990. During the 1970s the P & M mill cut well over one hundred thousand board feet of incense cedar "slats" a day. The wood was recut for pencil stock, and for years more than half the world's wood-cased pencils were clad in Mt. Shasta cedar. Roseburg Lumber Company closed its Mount Shasta mill in 1985 and donated the land to the city.Now, the only lumber mills in operation at the base of the mountain are a Roseburg mill in Weed and a P & M mill in McCloud.

Lumbering in the woods surrounding Mt. Shasta will probably never rebound to the level it attained in the early part of the twentieth century. The mature, old-growth forests are gone, and lumber companies in other areas of North America, particularly the southern states and the Pacific Northwest, are able to tree-farm timber more economically. The future of the industry in the Mt. Shasta area depends on the demand for wood products, the success of current reforestation programs, and the implementation of enlightened land-use planning and forest stewardship.

·87·

"Mt. Shasta" by Juan Wandesforde, 1863.

CHAPTER 7

NATIVE AMERICANS AND THEIR LEGENDS

THE NATIVE AMERICANS WHO LIVED IN WHAT IS NOW SISKIYOU COUNTY HAD TO ADAPT THEMSELVES TO DIVERSE GEO-GRAPHICAL CONDITIONS. In the low forests and deep river gorges of the Klamath Mountains, the dry Sacramento Valley, and the high plains of the Modoc Plateau, they lived peaceful, insular lives within sight of Mt. Shasta. The largest tribes were the Shasta, Karok, and Modoc to the north. The Wintun people occupied lands to the southwest, while the Achumawi and Atsugewi ranged to the east. A small tribe, the Okwanuchu, lived within the Sacramento and McCloud River watersheds, close to Mt. Shasta's southwestern flanks.

During the early part of the twentieth century, anthropologist Alfred L. Kroeber and ethnologist Roland B. Dixon made studies of the Native Americans living in California. Based upon very broad linguistic and cultural elements, Kroeber distin-guished major divisions among the tribes. He regarded those living around the base of Mt. Shasta to be situated on the edge of—and influenced by—several major cultures: the North Coast civilizations to the west and northwest, the central Californian tribes to the south and the high plains culture to the east.

Dixon carefully collected and recorded tribal myths and legends and found that Mt. Shasta was often an integral part of the mythology of the peoples of a large cultural sphere. There were legends of Coyote on Mt. Shasta, typical of cultures both in central California and northward. The personification of Wind, which was very common to the Northwest Coast tribes, was also often a factor in legends surrounding the mountain.

The California tribes have long traditions of oral history: tribal histories, legends, and tales have been handed down from

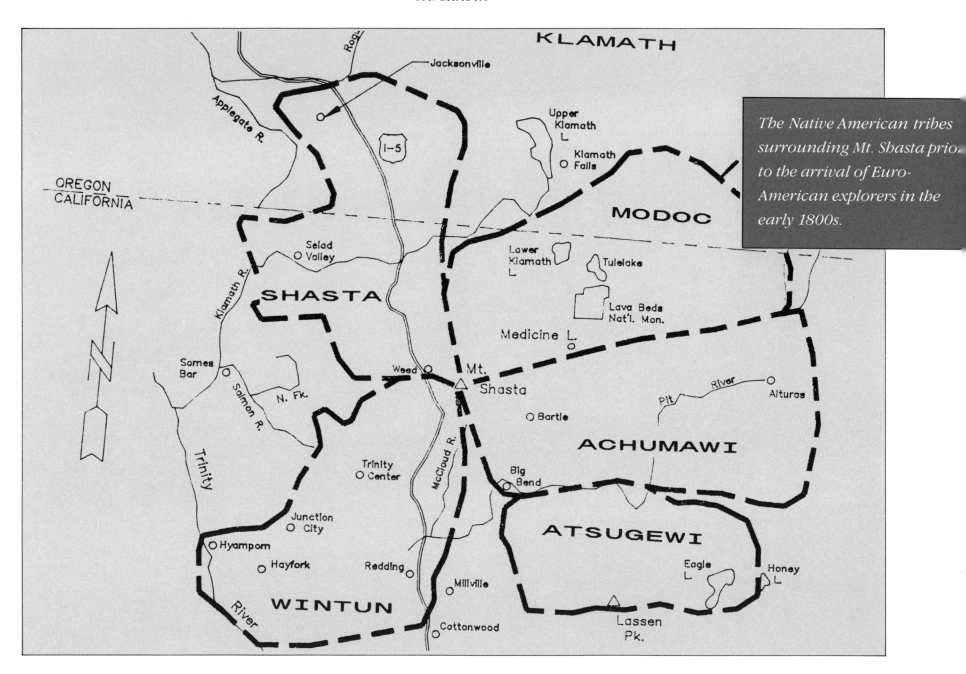

KLAMATH

Jacksonville

Applegate R.

I-5

Upper
Klamath
L.

Klamath
Falls

OREGON
CALIFORNIA

MODOC

Selad
Valley

Lower
Klamath
L.

Tulelake

SHASTA

Lava Beds
Nat'l. Mon.

Medicine L.

Klamath R.

Somes
Bar

Salmon R.

N. Fk.

Weed

Mt.
Shasta

Pit   River

Alturas

Bartle

ACHUMAWI

Trinity

McCloud R.

Trinity
Center

Big
Bend

Junction
City

ATSUGEWI

Hyampom

Hayfork

Redding

Eagle
L.

Honey
L.

Millville

WINTUN

River

Cottonwood

Lassen
Pk.

The Native American tribes surrounding Mt. Shasta prior to the arrival of Euro-American explorers in the early 1800s.

generation to generation with great accuracy. They were a way to record tribal history at a time when written history was unknown. Tribal members learned tales word for word from their elders; accuracy was never doubted, for deviations were forbidden. These rich and diverse heritages have been studied and well documented by anthropologists and ethnographers, so many legends survive to this day.

Joaquin Miller, the "Poet of the Sierras," lived for a time during the 1850s with the Native Americans of the Mt. Shasta region and recorded several of their tales. Miller wrote of the storytellers:

A storyteller is held in great repute; but he is not permitted to lie or romance under any circumstances. All he says must bear the stamp of truth, or he is disgraced forever. Telling stories, their history, traditions, travels, and giving and receiving lessons in geography, are their chief diversion around their camp and wigwam fires. At night, when no wars or excitement of any kind stirred the village, they would gather in the chief's or other great bark lodges around the fires, and tell and listen to stories; a red wall of men in a great circle, the women a little back, and the children still behind, asleep in the skins and blankets. How silent! You never hear but one voice at a time in an Indian village.

Mt. Shasta was the unmistakable physical and visual center of several tribes. It was customary for great peaks to be regarded by Native American peoples as the starting point of their many boundaries. And, in spite of the differences among tribes in locations, language, and tribal affiliations, Shasta was recognized by each in its own way as something of such immense grandeur that its existence could only be attributed to the Great Spirit, or Creator. The mountain, therefore, was also the tribes' spiritual center: it was held to be the Great Spirit's wigwam. The smoke and steam seen at the summit was the smoke-hole of the Spirit's lodge, as well as the entrance to the Earth.

Native American legends connected the material and spiritual worlds and described the powerful natural forces that people witnessed in their environment. Joaquin Miller recorded this tale of the creation of Mt. Shasta:

The Indians say the Great Spirit made this mountain first of all. Can you not see how it is? He first pushed down snow and ice from the skies through a hole which he made in the blue heavens by turning a stone round and round, till he made this great mountain, then he stepped out of the clouds on to the mountain top, and descended and planted the trees all around by putting his finger on the ground. The sun melted the snow, and the water ran down and nurtured the trees and made the rivers. After that he made the fish for the rivers out of the small end of his staff. He made the birds by blowing some leaves which he took up from the ground among the trees. After that he made the beasts out of the remainder of his stick, but made the grizzly bear out of the big end, and made him master over all the others. He made the grizzly so strong that he feared him himself, and would have to go up on the top of the mountain out of sight of the forest to sleep at night, lest the grizzly, who, as will be seen was much more strong and cunning then than now, should assail him in his sleep. Afterwards, the Great Spirit wishing to remain on earth, and make the sea and some more land, he converted Mt. Shasta by a great deal of labor into a wigwam, and built a fire in the center of it and made it a pleasant home. After that his family came down, and they all have lived in the mountain ever since. They say that before the white

·91·

man came they could see the fire ascending from the mountain by night and the smoke by day, every time they chose to look in that direction.

THE KAROK

Another tribe, the Karok, told a story about a great chief who had taken his people on a yearly pilgrimage to the Pacific Ocean until, finally, he grew too old to make the journey. Wishing to see the great ocean once more before he died, he instructed his people to build a mountain from whose top he might view the sea. His people willingly set about the task, gathering earth from the north in their baskets and dumping it in an ever-growing mound. When the hill was finally high enough for the chief to see the ocean, he shouted, "Stop! I can see it!" The workers dumped their remaining baskets of earth where they stood, thereby creating the hundreds of little hills north of the mountain in Shasta Valley.

THE GREAT FLOOD

Legends of a Great Flood and tales of cataclysmic endings and beginnings were also common throughout Native American cultures. Many tribes believed that before the first people were created, the world was inhabited by a race of animal-people. The Achumawi told of Hawk-Man, who, angered at the loss of his wives, put on his shaman's vestments and brought a great rain. All night it poured, and the water rose higher and higher. The other animals, fearing for their lives, killed Hawk-Man. After he had been slain the flood waters began to subside, but the animal-people found that all their fires had been put out and nothing could be cooked. Owl was sent to the top of Mt. Shasta to see if he could find any trace of fire—he did, and that is why we have fire today.

·92·

Joaquin Miller related another legend of the Great Flood, which involved Coyote, the shrewd trickster and people's perpetual nemesis: Coyote had been walking by a large body of water where an evil spirit lived. This spirit caused the water to rise up and cover Coyote, so Coyote shot the spirit with his bow and arrow and ran away. But the water followed him. He ran to higher ground, but still the water followed him. Finally, Coyote ran to the top of Mt. Shasta, where he made a fire on the only dry ground remaining. The other animals—Grizzly Bear, Deer, Gray Squirrel, Jack Rabbit, Badger, and Wolf—all saw the fire and swam to Mt. Shasta's summit, where they stayed until the flood was over. They then came down from the top of Mt. Shasta, scattered themselves far and wide, and became the ancestors of all the animal-people on Earth.

THE MODOC

The Modocs' account of their own creation also involves Mt. Shasta: Many thousands of snows ago there was a great storm about the summit of Mt. Shasta. The Great Spirit within sent his youngest daughter up to the hole in the top, bidding her to speak to the storm and tell it to be more gentle lest it blow the mountain over. He instructed her to do this hastily and not put her head out, otherwise the wind would catch her hair and blow her away. The girl hurried to the top and spoke to the storm, but never having seen the ocean where the wind was born, she put her head out for one brief look.

The storm caught her long red hair and carried her away, down the mountainside to the forest below. All of the land and forests, even down to the sea, were then possessed by the Grizzlies. They were not exactly beasts then, but creatures that walked on two legs, talked, and were covered with hair. At this time there was a family of Grizzlies living high in the forests of Mt. Shasta, close to the snow. The father Grizzly, returning to his cave with food, found the young girl under a fir tree shivering with fright and cold, her long hair trailing in the snow. He brought her home, where the mother Grizzly raised her as one of their own.

When the daughter of the Great Spirit was grown, she married the oldest Grizzly son. They were very happy and had many children. But, being part of the Great Spirit and part of the Grizzly bear, these children did not exactly resemble either of their parents, but somewhat of the nature and likeness of both: they were the first Modocs.

THE SHASTA

While many Native American tribes had only general tales about Mt. Shasta and its significance, storytellers of the Shasta tribe were more specific in their lore. One of their legends was about Thumb Rock, the craggy promontory at the eastern end of the Red Banks that is a familiar landmark to modern-day climbers of the mountain:

At the foot of the mountain lived a great chief and his peaceful tribe. The chief had a beautiful daughter sought by many fine young men. In those days a bride was purchased; the amount paid depended upon her social standing. Chief Big Rock of the Modoc tribe had paid for the daughter to be his bride. However, the girl was in love with Flying Eagle, the son of the tribal medicine man. The night before Chief Big Rock came for her, she and Flying Eagle fled. They walked all night toward the east, where they thought they would find safety with another tribe. It was foggy, and they couldn't see well, but they sensed they were climbing a hill. They climbed until the woman could go no farther, then stopped to rest under a giant rock. Several days later a guide was sent out by Chief Big Rock to look for the couple. He found them frozen, and reported that the maiden's thumbs were pointing outward. The giant rock they were under also looked like a thumb and was pointing the same way as the woman's. This story was told as a warning never to attempt to climb Mt. Shasta.

Shasta Native American woman, late 1890s.

COURTESY SISKIYOU COUNTY MUSEUM

·93·

HOT SPRINGS AND EARTHQUAKES

The hot sulphur springs near Mt. Shasta's summit are well known to climbers. These bubbling pools of mud and noxious sulphur fumes are a reminder that Shasta is a dormant volcano. Indeed, the recent eruption of Mount St. Helens in Washington State is proof that the sleeping giants of the Cascade Range are unpredictable and can awaken at any time. It is not known if the summit hot springs were more prolific in earlier times, or if the mountain spewed forth steam and fumes sufficient enough to waft down into the valleys where the Native Americans dwelled. Nevertheless, the Shasta tribe told a story explaining the sulphur springs and noxious fumes at Mt. Shasta's summit:

Long ago a tribe in the valley was having trouble preserving their meat and worried that they would not have enough during the cold winter months. They consulted with wise Old Yellow Jacket, who told them he knew a way to keep their meat from spoiling. Yellow Jacket had once seen a deer carcass preserved in glacial snow and ice high on Mt. Shasta. He told the people to kill as much as they could, then told his own tribe that if they carried the meat high on the mountain and buried it completely in the thick snow and ice, they could have the livers. The Yellow Jackets started their journey, but soon tired. They buried the meat in a place where there was only soft snow and even some bare earth. The meat rotted, and now climbers feel nauseated when they pass the area where the Yellow Jackets rested and buried the kill. The water running through the spoiled meat is the sulphur water of the summit hot springs.

Another reminder of Shasta's dynamic history has been periodic minor earthquake activity. These earthquakes reached a peak in recent times from 1978 through 1981 on Shasta's east side, and were the sort that indicate rising magma, or molten rock. Once again, it is not known what sort of volcanic or seismic activity early Native Americans witnessed, but the Wintu Tribe had a legend to explain the mountain's rumblings and shakings:

Long ago a very fierce and evil tribe lived on the east side of the mountain. This tribe, called the Bedit, was killing and eating all the Wintu they could capture. One night, two brave Wintu brothers crept into the Bedit's sweat-house and silently released all the Wintu captives. The brothers then tied together the long hair of the sleeping Bedits and piled great quantities of flammable pitchwood around the sides of the sweat house. Setting fire to the wood, the brothers stood by the smoke hole in the roof and struck down the Bedits as they tried to escape from the burning lodge. The two brothers beat all the Bedits back except one, who escaped to the top of Mt. Shasta. The brothers caught him and buried him in a deep cleft in the rock, where he can be heard and felt to this day, struggling to free himself.

THE LAND

In more recent times, the lands surrounding Mt. Shasta took on a different aspect to the local Native Americans. The gold rush brought catastrophic changes to their way of life. Ancestral lands were seized, and miners often shot the people for sport, usually with the tacit approval of government agents. Diseases like small-pox and tuberculosis decimated Native populations.

Anthropologist Alfred Kroeber estimated the Native American population in California was 133,000 in 1770. By 1910 it was 16,350. When the war with Mexico came to an end in the late 1840s, presidential envoys traveled to California to sign treaties with the Native Americans there. Gold-hungry settlers, afraid the pacts would allow the Native Americans to keep potentially valuable land, remonstrated vigorously to their Senators to vote against ratification of the treaties. Many California Natives consider the issue unresolved to this day.

The upper springs at Panther Meadows, near the end of Everitt Memorial Highway on Shasta's southwest flank, is still used by Flora Jones, a Wintun medicine woman, and others for medicinal purposes and prayer. Charlie Thom, a Karok medicine man, frequently conducts purification sweats at Sand Flat and other locations on the mountain. Thomas Doty of Ashland, Oregon, regularly recites the old stories and songs from northwestern tribes.

Klamath Native American, 1900.

COURTESY SISKIYOU COUNTY MUSEUM

COURTESY STEVE GERACE, 1990

CHAPTER 8

MODERN MYTHS AND THE SACRED MOUNTAIN

FOR CENTURIES MOUNTAINS HAVE REPRESENTED THE HIGHEST SACRED VALUES TO PEOPLES AND CULTURES: MOSES ON MT. SINAI, KAILAS TO HINDUS AND BUDDHISTS, FUJI TO THE JAPANESE, SAN FRANCISCO PEAKS TO THE HOPI AND NAVAJO. All of these mountains, and many others, are considered extraordinary by various cultures. Mountains have the power to evoke the mystical and dreamlike; they connect the earth—and people—to the sky, the abode of the gods. Metaphors and references to mountains throughout history are endless:

The 121st Psalm, "I will lift up mine eyes unto the hills, from whence cometh my help." Eighth-century Akahito wrote, "I will sing the praises of this exalted peak as long as I have breath." John Muir alluded to the mountains as his "cathedral." Fosco Maraini wrote, "In solitary, stony fastness among the mountains there is a strange market where you can barter the vortex of life for boundless bliss."

Native American legends were the precursors to modern myths about Mt. Shasta. The tribes used myth and legend to give meaning to their roots in creation and the phenomena they experienced. Euro-Americans, as they displaced the natives, used phenomena to support myth and chimera. Mt. Shasta remained the center and foundation for both peoples' legends and stories. The power of place, in this case Mt. Shasta, was the catalyst causing the myths to develop and flow.

Mt. Shasta, with its frequent storms and strange clouds, stands alone, as striking in its isolation today as it was centuries ago. Gazing at the mountain, one succumbs easily to fantasy and can almost reach across the centuries to the makers of the ancient myths.

FREDERICK SPENCER OLIVER AND PHYLOS

One of the earliest recorded Euro-American legends regarding Mt. Shasta began when Yreka teenager Frederick Spencer Oliver was helping mark the boundaries of his family's mining claim during the summer of 1883. As the young man drove wooden stakes along a survey line, he jotted down the number and location of each stake in a notebook. Evidently, as he took up his pencil to enter the information, his hand began to write uncontrollably.

Terrified, he ran two miles home to his parents. His mother fetched more writing paper, and Frederick continued to write until the strange force left his hand and arm. Over the next three years his hand would periodically be seized with the unusual force, and he would slowly write one or more pages. He finished a manuscript in 1895 under the title, *A Dweller on Two Planets*. The book became one of the first American occult classics and was followed by an equally popular sequel, *An Earth Dweller's Return*. (Entertainer Shirley MacLaine's bestselling book *Out on a Limb*, in which she recounts her spiritual odyssey, contains the story of her visit to a Hong Kong metaphysical bookstore, where a book mysteriously toppled off a shelf and into her hands. The book was *A Dweller on Two Planets*.)

In describing his writing, Oliver claimed that he had been chosen amanuensis, or secretary, to the Lemurian spirit Phylos, and that the book had been dictated to him through "automatic writing." Oliver claimed that Phylos, who lived during several previous incarnations on Atlantis, took him to mysterious temples and elaborate dwelling places of a mystic brotherhood within Mt. Shasta. He wrote that the interior of the mountain contained a labyrinth of great corridors with walls of polished jewels and floors carpeted with fur. The entrance to Mt. Shasta's inner sanctum was supposedly by a clear pool near a branch of the McCloud River on the mountain's east side. He wrote:

> We recline on the brink of a deep blue crystal pool, idly casting pebbles into the image of a tall basalt cliff reflected from the mirror-calm surface. What secrets perchance are about us? We do not know as we lie there, our bodies resting, our souls filled with peace, nor do we know until many years are passed out through the back door of time that that tall basalt cliff conceals a doorway. We do not suspect this, nor that a long tunnel stretches away, far into the interior of majestic Shasta. Wholly unthought is that there lie at the tunnel's far end vast apartments, the home of a mystic brotherhood, whose occult arts hollowed that tunnel and mysterious dwelling.

Oliver concluded *A Dweller on Two Planets* with a cryptic caveat:

> Once I was there, friend, casting pebbles
> in the stream's deep pool; yet it was then hid,
> for only a few are privileged. And departing,
> the spot was forgotten, and today, unable as anyone who reads this, I cannot tell its place. Does it
> truly exist? Shasta is a true guardian and silently
> towers, giving no sign of that within its breast.
> But there is a key. The one who first conquers
> self, Shasta will not deny.

1938 advertisement for a book offering to explain the mystery of the lost race of Lemuria dwelling within Mt. Shasta.

LOST CONTINENTS

Lemurians, Atlanteans, and other lost races sequestered within Mt. Shasta are often-told stories. Supposedly, Lemuria was once a great continent in the area now covered by the Pacific Ocean. The continent's eastern shore had once been part of the present states of California, Oregon, and Washington, separated from the rest of North America by a large inland sea. Indeed, science supports this theory to the extent that there is the remnant of an inland sea—the Great Salt Lake—in Utah. Geologists and paleontologists are also in agreement that oceans did cover much of the western half of the United States at one time.

Lemuria is said to have disappeared into the Pacific during a cataclysm that changed the geography of the entire globe. Some Lemurian people migrated east when their continent began to sink and made their way to Mt. Shasta. Because of their very advanced knowledge of science, energy, and cosmic powers, the Lemurians fashioned huge caverns within the mountain and were self-sustaining in every respect.

Another mysterious race said to be living within Mt. Shasta is the Yaktayvians, reputed to be the greatest bellmakers in the world. Using their mastery over sound and vibrations, the Yaktayvians used their bells and chimes to hollow out underground cities and produce light and power. Great transparent bells, invisible to mortals, are used to protect the secret mountainside entrances to their caverns.

In 1931 Harve Spencer Lewis, founder of the Rosicrucian Order in San Jose, California, published *Lemuria: Lost Continent of the Pacific* under the pseudonym Wishar S. Cerve. He claimed the book was based on long-lost Asian manuscripts and archives and in it detailed the origin and fall of Lemuria as long as five million years ago. Cerve recounted tales of strange-looking, robed persons emerging from the forests and coming into nearby towns surrounding Mt. Shasta to trade gold nuggets for supplies:

> These odd looking persons were not only peculiar in their dress and different in attire from any costume ever seen on the American Indian, and especially the California Indian, but distinctive in features and complexion; tall, graceful and agile, having the appearance of being quite old and yet exceedingly virile.

A protrusion in the center of their very high foreheads was said to be a special organ enabling them to communicate by telepathy. When approached by townspeople, the Lemurians would apparently vanish into thin air.

The Rosicrucians sold *Lemuria: Lost Continent of the Pacific* for $2.30, "complete with all necessary maps, tables, charts, and strange symbols," and the book enjoyed wide popularity during the 1930s. Letters arrived at the Shasta National Forest offices and local chambers of commerce from throughout the United States and abroad asking about the Lemurians, and each summer amateur archaeologists and searchers visited Mt. Shasta looking for evidence of the evasive lost race. Newspaper reporters naturally visited Mt. Shasta, drawn by the wealth of mysterious stories emanating from the area, but none of them found storekeepers who had actually seen Lemurians, nor did they find any secret entrances on the mountain's flanks.

Nevertheless, the stories continued. Unscrupulous promoters, who saw the opportunity to capitalize on the attention, offered tours and special retreats to Mt. Shasta. Often exorbitantly expensive, the tours promised everything from miraculous healing waters to special preparations and instructions guaranteeing acceptance into the great secret temples within the mountain. In 1935 the Rosicrucian Order distanced itself from the "societies responsible for the exaggerated and ridiculous claims that abound about Mt. Shasta" with this disclaimer:

> We are oftentimes amused by the rumors that we originated these tales or accepted them as facts. The book merely relates these legends. We are no more responsible for the facts than is the publisher who publishes "Anderson's Fairy Tales," or the "Arabian Nights."

The following year the Rosicrucians announced that excessive publicity caused the Lemurians to abandon Mt. Shasta in favor of more secretive locations.

Shasta's lost-race legends were carried a step further when "Dr. Doreal" of the "Brotherhood of the White Temple, Inc." in Sedalia, Colorado, claimed to have visited the mountain's secret inner abodes in the 1930s. Doreal, who published several occult booklets, departed from the Lemurian legends, claiming, instead, that Mt. Shasta was inhabited by Atlanteans. Doreal contended that Lemuria sank beneath the ocean when it was defeated in a great war with Atlantis. Mt. Shasta's Atlanteans were entrusted with guarding several million malevolent Lemurians imprisoned beneath the earth's surface—Lemurians whose knowledge of destructive forces was so terrible that it would be too dangerous to release them to wander the earth again.

GOLDEN CITIES

In the early 1920s, Professor Edgar Larkin, an astronomer who supposedly directed the Mt. Lowe observatory in Southern California, said he saw strange lights on Mt. Shasta. Larkin was atop an unnamed Northern California peak testing a new terrestrial lens on his telescope and had trained it on Mt. Shasta in order to calibrate a distance-measuring scale. He focused the telescope on Shasta's eastern slopes, expecting to see only forests, and was astounded to observe a glimmering gold-tinted dome rising above the trees. As the sun moved across the sky, Larkin saw two more domes. He returned to the telescope after sunset and found the domes glowing softly, even though there was no moon in the night sky at the time. Larkin claimed to have climbed Mt. Shasta with a small group in order to find the mysterious golden temples. By his accounts they found a hidden canyon high on Shasta's east side with lush, tropical vegetation and a warm climate.

Dr. Larkin's fantastic story—often taking on embellished forms—was widely circulated for years in Rosicrucian literature, Doreal's booklets, and the popular mystery "pulps" of the 1930s and 1940s. Some accounts credited Larkin with viewing Shasta from Southern California, a distance of nearly 800 miles. Dr. William Bridge Cooke, Mt. Shasta's preeminent botanist, researched some of the details of Larkin's story during the summer of 1940. Cooke could not find any listing for a Mt. Lowe observatory, but did find a Mt. Lowe 3 miles west of the famous Mt. Wilson observatory above Pasadena, California. Evidently, a small observatory had been operated in conjunction with a tourist inn on Mt. Lowe, but it had burned down in the late 1930s. Articles occasionally appeared with Larkin's name, after his first disclosure of Shasta's golden cities, but his whereabouts were thereafter unknown.

THE I AM ACTIVITY

The I AM Activity, or Saint Germain Foundation, is an organization with worldwide membership that began when the group's founder, Guy W. Ballard, claimed to have had an encounter with the "Ascended Master" Saint Germain on the slopes of Mt. Shasta in 1930. Ballard came to the area on a mining engineering job and frequently spent time hiking through Mt. Shasta's forests and meadows to ponder rumors and stories of an ancient "Brotherhood of Mt. Shasta" he had heard about.

As Ballard recounted his experiences in his book *Unveiled Mysteries* and other writings, he stopped one day at a mountain spring for a drink and felt a strange electric current pass through his body. He turned around and was astonished to see a man who addressed him: "My Brother, if you will hand me your cup, I will give you a much more refreshing drink than spring water." Ballard drank the liquid and described the moment:

A 1937 painting of Saint Germain.

COURTESY LEROY FOSTER

"While the taste was delicious, the electrical vivifying effect in my mind and body made me gasp with surprise. I did not see him put anything into the cup, and I wondered what was happening." Later, the man—who was actually Saint Germain—offered Ballard some small cakes which he ate. "Immediately, I felt a quickening, tingling sensation through my entire body—a new sense of health and clearness of mind. Saint Germain seated himself beside me and my instruction began." Ballard wrote that for the next several weeks he had experiences with Saint Germain that included ethereal travel to the world's ancient civilizations and cities, teachings of universal truths, and the accompaniment of a beautiful panther during his walks on Mt. Shasta.

Ballard returned to his native Chicago and in the next few years wrote several books under the nom de plume Godfre Ray King, describing other meetings with Saint Germain and the arcane teachings and instructions the Ascended Master had directed him to record. Ballard claimed that he was a messenger for a group of beings known as Ascended Masters, which included Christ, Moses, Saint Francis, Buddha, and Saint Germain and were here to help humankind. In 1933 Ballard told small groups of friends about his experiences, and in less than a year acquired a large, devoted following. By 1935 he and his wife began touring the United States, appearing before crowds of seven and eight thousand people nightly in halls like the Los Angeles Shrine, and San Francisco's Scottish Rite auditorium. By the late 1930s they had appeared in most major U.S. cities and had sold several hundred thousand books.

Ballard described the basic teachings of Saint Germain to be that the goal of life is "ascension," or union with God. The key, according to the teachings, was that every individual has a "Mighty I AM Presence" of God that can be called forth for assistance at any time. At various times Ballard claimed that through his contacts with Saint Germain, dangerous threats to the freedom of America and humankind were averted by powerful "decrees," or affirmations issued by him and other members of the movement.

When Ballard died in 1939, the organization was taken over by his wife, Edna, who continued to conduct classes and meetings she said were dictated and influenced by Saint Germain. During the 1940s the organization weathered accusations of impropriety and fraud in a case that went all the way to the U.S. Supreme Court. In 1948 the organization purchased Shasta Springs, an historic old railroad resort overlooking the Sacramento River between Dunsmuir and the town of Mount Shasta. Considerable investment went into improving the facilities, and today more than 450 members can stay at one time for meetings, classes, and other gatherings.

In 1950 the group bought land at the east side of the town of Mount Shasta to construct an outdoor amphitheater for their annual pageant. The pageant features a dramatic reenactment of the life of Christ and is presented each August at the conclusion of a month-long conclave at the Shasta Springs retreat. The pageant has been open to the general public since 1956, and crowds of several thousand people, some from as far as Australia, South Africa, and Europe, regularly attend the event.

The I AM pageant, depicting the life of Christ, is performed each summer at the Saint Germain Foundation amphitheater in the town of Mount Shasta.

When Edna Ballard died in 1971, leadership of the organization reverted to a governing board of directors with headquarters in Chicago. The membership of the I AM Activity is currently between four and five thousand people in nearly two dozen countries; several thousand additional people who participate in the group on an irregular basis are considered secondary members. The I AM Activity has achieved a longevity and level of acceptance by the local community beyond that of any other religious or esoteric groups associated with Mt. Shasta. To the members of the I AM Activity, Mt. Shasta will always be very special because it was the place chosen by Saint Germain to deliver his teachings to humanity through founder Guy Ballard.

THE HARMONIC CONVERGENCE

Mt. Shasta continues to attract attention as a hallowed place and sacred mountain. The Harmonic Convergence gathering on the mountain on August 16 and 17, 1987, was part of a worldwide event. The occasion was intended to herald a new phase of world cooperation and harmony among the planet's peoples and its environment, and was coordinated at the same time as other global-communication events, such as Hands Across America, Space Bridges, and World Peace Day.

One of the organizers of the event, author and philosopher Jose Arguelles, cited ancient prophesies in the Mayan calendar and special astrological alignments of the planets occurring around the time of the Convergence that would help influence a world shift in human consciousness. Mt. Shasta was chosen as one of the gathering points because it was considered among the most sacred mountains on Earth. Between four and five thousand people, from as far away as Australia and Europe, gathered above Panther meadows at the site of the old Mt. Shasta Ski Bowl to greet the sunrise and participate in music, meditations, seminars, and Native American ceremonies.

Tai Situpa Rinpoche conducting a special Tibetan environmental ceremony at Bunny Flat on Mt. Shasta in 1989.

TIBETAN LAMAS

In October 1989 Tai Situpa Rinpoche, one of Tibet's most revered lamas, included a special Tibetan ceremony on Mt. Shasta in the itinerary of his round-the-world "Pilgrimage for Active Peace." Rinpoche is believed by his followers to be the twelfth incarnation of the Tai Situpa, a lineage that is traced to one of the chief disciples of Gotama Buddha. Exiled from his Tibetan homeland when he was six years old, Rinpoche has since toured the world, speaking on multicultural cooperation, spirituality, and building bridges between nations.

Prior to coming to Mt. Shasta he met with Pope John Paul II at the Vatican and several Nobel laureates in Scotland, and hosted a special celebration for the Dalai Lama in San Francisco to celebrate the Tibetan leader's acceptance of the Nobel Peace Prize.

·103·

Several hundred people gathered at Bunny Flat on Mt. Shasta on October 18 to participte in a traditional Tibetan ceremony to promote harmony between envorinomental forces and human activity. Tibetan horns were sounded to announce the arrival of Rinpoche and several other lamas, who began the ceremony with prayer. A small choir of Tibetan refugees sang their national anthem and carried prayer flags high up Shasta's Green Butte ridge to flutter in the wind. At the end of the beautiful fall day, Rinpoche said:

> We should thank the spirits of this place, they have given us a perfect day; they recognize our intentions.

Rinpoche was asked why he came to Mt. Shasta. He said:

> It was about three or four years ago that I flew from Europe to San Francisco direct. At that time I saw Mt. Shasta from my airplane. I was amazed about the majestic appearance of the mountain. As a Tibetan we have an explanation for the meaning of the shape . . . it's like somebody made it, somebody made it with lots of planning. It looked perfect! It stayed in my mind and I felt that one day I must go and do a traditional Tibetan ceremony there to offer prayers for the enviroment.

It cannot be denied that Mt. Shasta is a special, powerful place that represents many feelings to many people. To some, the feeling is intangible, ephemeral, and beyond words. Many modern-day artists have painted Mt. Shasta in a style, often referred to as "visionary art," that gives expression to some of the mystical and fantastic feeings the mountain evokes. This style probably has its roots with Michelangelo, Leonardo da Vinci, and other great artists who envisioned the ethereal and fantastic in their view of religious and spiritual universality.

The famous Russian painter Nikolay Roerich brought this form, emphasizing mountains, into world culture at the beginning of the twentieth century with fanciful, imaginative scenes of the Himalayas. Mt. Shasta has been the backdrop and focus for angels, spirits, and spaceships, and many well-known artists, such as Cheryl Yambrach Rose, Gilbert Williams, Rodney Birkett, Leonardo Gonzales, and Andralaria, have painted their impressions of the mountain.

"The Awakened Golden Solar Angel" by Cheryl Yambrach Rose, 1990.

COURTESY THE ARTIST

Today Mt. Shasta is surrounded by groups like the I AM Activity, Planetary Citizens, Brotherhood of the White Temple, Radiant School of Seekers and Servers, League of Voluntary Effort (LOVE), and a Zen monastery, among many others, which have felt a calling to locate near it. Many individuals who live in the area speak of the mountain as a power source or a spiritual focus in their lives. The myths and legends surrounding the mountain add another facet to a place that, however defined, is seen and felt in many more ways than most mountains.

To many, Mt. Shasta represents a special place that bridges words and feelings, the physical and the spritual, the earthly and the mythological. Typical of the feelings of many are these words, written in the summit register book by an anonymous climber in 1971:

> When I am here on this mountain I am reminded that there is greater significance to this physical existence than what meets the eye, and I am turned into my own revelation of Godliness.

Mt. Shasta often casts a pyramid shadow at sunrise
that can be seen from the summit. Strange clouds, shadows,
and sunsets add to the mystical aura of the mountain.

·105·

Woodblock print by unknown artist.

Appeared around the time of John Muir's first Mt. Shasta National Park proposals.

CHAPTER 9

MT. SHASTA PRESERVATION EFFORTS

THE IDEA OF A MT. SHASTA NATIONAL PARK BEGAN IN 1888 WITH A PROPOSAL FROM THE GREAT AMERICAN NATURALIST, JOHN MUIR. In the popular magazine *Picturesque California,* which Muir edited, he wrote:

> The Shasta region may be reserved as a National Park, with special reference to the preservation of its fine forests and game. This should by all means be done. . . . The Shasta region is still a fresh unspoiled wilderness, accessible and available for travelers of every kind and degree. Would it not then be a fine thing to set it apart like the Yellowstone and Yosemite as a National Park for the welfare and benefit of all mankind, preserving its fountains and forests and all its glad life in primeval beauty? Very little of the region can ever be more valuable for any other use—certainly not for gold nor for grain. No private right or interest need suffer, and thousands yet unborn would come from far and near and bless the country for its wise and benevolent forethought.

The first attempt to actually create a Mt. Shasta National Park was a proposal by the Sisson Promotion Association, an organization of Northern California business people very much like today's chambers of commerce. The proposal was adopted on February 14, 1912—coincidentally the eighty-fifth anniversary of Peter Skene Ogden's historic, if not actual, discovery of the mountain. The Sisson Promotion Association's interest in a national park recognized, of course, the extraordinary natural beauty of the mountain, but astutely appreciated the commercial possibilities as well.

The Panama-Pacific International Exposition, celebrating the opening of the Panama Canal, was scheduled for San Francisco in 1915. The association foresaw thousands of tourists coming to Northern California—many of whom, they hoped, would want to visit California's famous Mt. Shasta—and urged that "Mt. Shasta . . . together with such additional territory as may be determined, be declared a National Park and maintained as such."

Enthusiasm and interst in the new Mt. Shasta Park proposal grew rapidly, and in less than two weeks after the Sisson Promotion Association's plans were adopted, copies were sent to President Taft, Secretary of the Interior Walter Fisher, and California's Congressional delegation. Accordingly, on March 26, 1912, John E. Raker, Representative from California's second Congressional District, introduced H.R. 22353 to the sixty-second Congress: "A bill to set apart certain lands in the State of California as a public park, to be known as the Mount Shasta National park, in the Sierra Nevada Mountains, in the State of California, and for other purposes." The bill called for a park of 206,197 acres (more than 320 square miles). It made its way through the required Congressional committees, but the sixty-second Congress adjourned before it could be scheduled for vote.

Raker introduced the Shasta National Park bill again, now called H.R. 53, early in the sixty-third Congress. The bill quickly passed through the Public Lands Committee and was favorably reported upon by new Secretary of the Interior, Franklin Lane. This time an unforeseen turn of events entered the picture. Raker, almost as an afterthought, had introduced another bill, to create a Mt. Lassen National Park, at the same time as the Shasta bill. Only a few weeks after the introduction of the two bills—and while they were being scheduled for vote—Mt. Lassen awoke from dormancy and erupted. Suddenly, Mt. Lassen was the only active volcano in the continental United States, and pictures of its fiery lava and towering clouds of smoke were on the front page of every American newspaper. Raker then

68TH CONGRESS
2D SESSION

H. R. 12408

IN THE HOUSE OF REPRESENTATIVES

FEBRUARY 24, 1925

Mr. RAKER introduced the following bill; which was referred to the Committee on the Public Lands and ordered to be printed

---

A BILL

To establish the Mount Shasta National Park in the State of California

1 Be it enacted by the Senate and House of Representa-

2 tives of the United States of America in Congress assembled,

3 That there is hereby reserved and withdrawn from settle-

4 ment. occupation, or disposal under the laws of the United

5 States. and dedicated and set apart as a public park for the

6 benefit and enjoyment of the people, under the name of

7 the "Mount Shasta National Park," a tract of land in the

8 State of California, within the boundaries particularly de-

9 scribed as follows, to wit: All of township 40 north, range

10 2 west; all of township 41 north. range 2 west; all of

concentrated his energy on the Lassen bill (finally signed by President Wilson in 1916), meanwhile forgetting the Shasta bill.

The idea for a Mt. Shasta National Park languished for more than ten years after the 1914 failure until Raker, still in office, introduced a third Shasta bill in 1925. H.R. 12408, introduced in the final days of the sixty-eighth Congress, was "for the purpose of having discussion during the summer vacation, so that when Congress reconvenes the bill can be re-introduced with prospects of its early report and favorable consideration by the Congress." This time the bill bogged down on its journey through the House and never came before the Public Lands Committee for discussion or the full legislature for vote. At the time, the Southern Pacific and Central Pacific railroads—the principal private land holders on Mt. Shasta—were willing to sell their lands for $2 an acre. Raker died on January 22, 1926, ending the most sustained legislative effort for the creation of a Mt. Shasta National Park.

After Raker's several attempts on behalf of Shasta failed, his successor, Congressman Harry L. Englebright, tried to generate interest for the new park. But now, the political climate had changed in a way that made the creation of new national parks more difficult. The nation's cattle industry, fearful of being excluded from public grazing lands, lobbied angrily through their representatives against any new national parks. At the same time, national parks were also recognized as commercial gold mines, and jealousy developed between various states having lands of potential park caliber. California, already having four national parks, was opposed by several less fortunate states from having any new ones. The nation's young National Park Service was also forming new critera and guidelines for setting aside lands, and their policies were not favorable for a new Shasta park.

In 1929 A. E. Demaray, assistant director of the National Park Service, defined his agency's policy for considering new parks:

> They must be of sufficient size to allow the development of tourist facilities on a large and comprehensive scale and also should not duplicate the major characteristics of any existing national park.

The final gasp in nearly two decades of attempting to create a Mt. Shasta National Park was extinguished by the Park Service's new guidelines. There was nothing on Mt. Shasta, they decided, that was not already duplicated on Washington State's Mt. Rainier, already a national park.

Various suggestions were offered during the following years as substitutes for a Mt. Shasta National Park, such as a state park or national monument, but none found the necessary support. In 1928 and 1929 M. Hall McAllister, the prominent San Francisco judge responsible for building the Sierra Club's Shasta Alpine Lodge at Horse Camp, lobbied unsuccessfully for a state park. During the 1930s conservationist William G. Schulz proposed a Mt. Shasta National Park that also included Castle Crags to the south and some of the rugged lava fields to the northeast. Shasta was overlooked again, but a twist of irony saw the establishment of Castle Crags State Park and Lava Beds National Monument. Until the 1984 establishment of the Mt. Shasta Wilderness Area, Shasta was the only major Cascade peak not to have received national park or wilderness designation.

·109·

Original 1925 bill to create a Mt. Shasta National Park.

THE MT. SHASTA WILDERNESS AREA

In 1903 John Muir escorted President Theodore Roosevelt through Yosemite, the showpiece of America's national parks. Muir said, "I never before had so interesting, hearty, and manly a companion." Roosevelt replied, "John Muir talked even better than he wrote." The following day Roosevelt directed Secretary of the Interior, Ethan Hitchcock, to extend the Sierra Forest Reserve northward all the way to Mt. Shasta. "We are not building this country of ours for a day, it is to last through the ages," said Roosevelt.

Gifford Pinchot, the nation's first Forest Service chief, had presented his ideas on the preservation of forests to a receptive Roosevelt. Both the Shasta and Trinity Forest Reserves (later changed to "National Forests") were created by Roosevelt's Presidential Proclamation of 1905. When they were originally established, the Shasta Forest contained more than a million and a half acres, the Trinity Forest slightly less. The two forests were consolidated into the Shasta-Trinity National Forest in 1954 with administrative headquarters located in Redding, California.

The conflict between preserving and exploiting the nation's public lands and forests had already simmered for nearly a hundred years when Senator Hubert Humphrey introduced the first wilderness bill in 1956. The Forest Service, fearful that preserving wilderness would override other forest uses, suggested a modified bill emphasizing five major aspects of public land—timber, grazing, water, wildlife, and recreation—each issue receiving equal priority. Humphrey's bill, containing an amendment stating that the creation and maintenance of wilderness areas was consistent with the provisions of the legislation, became the Multiple Use-Sustained Yield Act and was signed into law on June 12, 1960, by President Dwight Eisenhower.

On September 3, 1964, Congress passed the Wilderness Act. This legislation established a National Wilderness Preservation System comprising certain federal lands and outlined standards for protecting and managing these special areas, "where the earth and its community of life are untrammeled by man; where man himself is a visitor who does not remain." The act also specified procedures for acquiring new lands, stating that "it is the policy of Congress to secure for the American people of present and future generations, the benefits of an enduring resource of wilderness." Under the Wilderness Act, remaining unroaded, untrammeled public wildlands designated by the Forest Service were to receive interim protection until Congress determined if and when they would be designated as wilderness areas. Areas not selected would revert back to the Forest Service's multiple-use category.

In 1973 the Forest Service identified more than twenty roadless regions in California, including Mt. Shasta, for study as potential wilderness areas under their first Roadless Area Review and Evaluation program, or RARE I, as it was popularly called. A second review program, RARE II, was initiated in 1977. By 1978 a draft environmental statement for a Mt. Shasta Wilderness Area was completed by a Forest Service team of specialists in recreation, timber, biology, economics, and other disciplines. The Forest Service recommended a 24,760-acre Mt. Shasta Wilderness Area, mostly on the mountain's upper slopes.

John Muir guided President Theodore Roosevelt through Yosemite in 1903 and lobbied for additional wilderness lands and National Parks. Shortly after, Roosevelt ordered the Sierra Forest Reserves extended to Mt. Shasta.

COURTESY LIBRARY OF CONGRESS

The Forest Service anticipated only benign controversy over its wilderness recommendation but was severely taken to task by environmentalists, timber interests, county governments, and a ski area—all in sharp conflict with each other over special interests. Several counties, including Siskiyou County, where Mt. Shasta is located, went on record against any new wilderness, fearful that timber-producing lands taken out of production would reduce their share of forest reserve funds. Ski Shasta Corporation, which operated a small ski area above Panther Meadows at the end of the Everitt Memorial Highway on the mountain, was planning a major expansion to the west. Environmental groups, already unhappy at what they considered a "rock and ice" wilderness proposal, objected to the planned ski expansion into the Sand Flat-Cascade Gulch area, which contains the mountain's largest pure stand of Shasta red fir and is very popular with hikers and cross-country skiers. More than nine thousand acres of private land had to be acquired to create the proposed wilderness area. This land, owned by several timber companies, required very sensitive and complex negotiations in order to exchange it for Forest Service land of equal value.

To many lovers of Mt. Shasta, the Forest Service wilderness proposal was a classic example of too little, too late, and a sad commentary on the failure to preserve an extraordinary mountain. The Forest Service admitted that more than 90 percent of the mountain's forests had already been logged. Their proposed twenty-four-thousand-acre wilderness recommendation was a striking contrast to John Muir's vision of a three- to four-hundred-thousand-acre national park, or Congressman John Raker's two-hundred-thousand-acre proposal. The Mt. Shasta Resource Council (MSRC), a grass-roots environmental organization, countered the Forest Service's wilderness recommendation with a proposal calling for forty-one thousand acres of wilderness, including as much of the remaining Shasta red fir forests as possible. The MSRC also introduced a new concept,

·111·

U. S. Forest Service, Mt. Shasta office, 1920s.

COURTESY SISKIYOU COUNTY MUSEUM

a "wilderness recovery zone," suggesting an additional thirty-two thousand acres of logged and partially logged lands be allowed to revert to a natural state, then be added to the initial wilderness.

The controversy over Mt. Shasta mirrored a much larger conflict in California and the rest of the nation. The Forest Service had already been taken to court and forced to reevaluate qualifying wilderness lands that it had neglected or overlooked in its initial studies. RARE II, the second generation of wilderness recommendations, also stirred heated controversy along the conservation-exploitation spectrum, and it was feared that the entire review process would have to be repeated a third time.

Meanwhile, Congress kept a close watch on the Mt. Shasta issue. The controversy caused Chair John Sieberling to bring his entire Congressional Public Lands Subcommittee to Mt. Shasta in June 1979 for field hearings on the complex dispute. The subcommittee members, most of whom had never seen Mt. Shasta, were impressed. Several years after the visit, Andrew Wiessner, chief counsel to the subcommittee, recalled the hearings and the mountain:

> It was more than just a large mountain,
> more than just a wilderness and more than just
> another ski area. It had a spiritual value and soul
> all of its own and a loyal following unlike any
> other area in the country that we visited . . . and
> we visited hundreds of areas.

The following summer Sieberling spent part of his legislative recess backpacking on the mountain.

In 1980 California Congressman Philip Burton introduced his California Wilderness Act, an omnibus bill for all of California, in an attempt to avoid becoming bogged down with individual bills for several wilderness areas. Burton, one of the most tireless champions of wilderness ever to serve in Congress, called in his sweeping bill for the addition of fifty-seven new roadless areas to the National Wilderness Preservation System. A 37,000-acre area of Mt. Shasta was included, and the bill referred to the mountain as "the most prominent, and arguably the most spectacular, geological feature in northern California." The bill passed the House in 1980, and again in 1981, but failed to pass the Senate. In early February 1983 Burton introduced a third bill, H.R. 1437, the Californian Wilderness Act of 1983. He died unexpectedly soon after the bill was introduced, but the House of Representatives passed the "Burton Bill" as a tribute to his memory on April 12, 1983.

The issue, however, was not over. California Senator Alan Cranston, previously a strong advocate of wilderness areas, refused to support the Burton Bill unless potential ski areas were excluded, specifically on Mt. Shasta. Cranston had already angered the California ski industry for his failure to support a proposed new ski area at Mineral King in the Sierra Nevada a few years earlier. He visited Mt. Shasta several times to broker a boundary compromise that excluded potential ski sites, and the bill finally passed the Senate.

President Ronald Reagan signed the California Wilderness Act, including the Mt. Shasta Wilderness Area, into law on September 28, 1984, nearly one hundred years after John Muir, alarmed at the demise of Shasta's forests, first suggested protecting the magnificent mountain.

COURTESY CH2M HILL

CHAPTER 10

MT. SHASTA IN RECENT TIMES

TODAY, LESS THAN TWO CENTURIES SINCE ITS DISCOVERY BY EURO-AMERICANS, MT. SHASTA EXISTS, IN A SENSE, IN TWO WORLDS. It is rooted in an ancient past, evidenced by vestigial forests, active glaciers, and debris from great lava flows of a proto-Mt. Shasta. But it is also surrounded with the trappings of twentieth-century civilization, including interstate highways, towns, and environmental impact and controversy.

SKIING AND ENVIRONMENTAL CONCERNS

Conflict and controversy over skiing on Mt. Shasta have continued since the 1984 California Wilderness Act deleted from wilderness protection all potential sites for downhill ski development on the mountain. Soon after the Mt. Shasta Wilderness Area was established the Forest Service issued a prospectus for 1,670 acres on Shasta's southwest slopes as feasible for a ski area.

Downhill skiing returned to Mt. Shasta in 1985 with the opening of Mt. Shasta Ski Park.

The winning bidder on the prospectus was the Mt. Shasta Ski Area (MSSA). Its original plan included a village complex, condominiums, hotels, ski lifts, gondolas, a golf course, and an RV park. The only other bidder was a local company on the verge of opening Mt. Shasta Ski Park, a ski area situated on private land adjacent to the Forest Service permit area.

Several prominent environmental groups, as well as California's attorney general, John Van de Kamp, concerned that the cumulative impact and lack of study of such a large development failed to follow environmental laws, began a series of appeals of the project. After issuance of the final environmental impact statement in 1990, Forest Service chief F. Dale Robertson made the unprecedented ruling that no further appeals would be allowed, and the ski area was approved. In March 1991 a coalition of environmental groups that included the California Wilderness Coalition, The Wilderness Society, and the Sierra Club's Mother Lode Chapter sued the Forest Service for failing to follow NEPA (National Environmental Policy Act) guidelines. The case was heard in a federal district court in August 1991, and a ruling was handed down authorizing another round of appeals. At this writing, the appeals are pending a decision from the Forest Service.

During the late 1980s the ideas of a Mt. Shasta National Park and other forms of long-term protection attracted renewed interest. The Save Mount Shasta group and the Mount Shasta Protection Committee began organizing efforts to limit large-scale development and further logging on the mountain, and to secure protected status for areas on the mountain and surrounding lands previously excluded from the Mt. Shasta Wilderness Area. Another of the main objectives of these groups was to call attention to traditional Native American relationships to Mt. Shasta. In March 1991 the California State Office of Historic Preservation ordered a study of Mt. Shasta for sites that could be eligible for listing in the National Register of Historic Places.

Each summer thousands of people attempt the climb to Shasta's summit. Although accurate statistics are difficult to keep, the Forest Service reports that at least five thousand try the climb annually, and fewer than 50 percent are successful. Shasta's popularity with climbers and hikers also has a negative side: an average of one fatality per year has taken place on the mountain during the last decade. The growth of recreation on the mountain has caused Forest Service planners to begin looking at different recreation management strategies. Their Mt. Shasta Wilderness Management Plan, and a long-ranged Forest Plan for the entire Shasta-Trinity National Forest are pending.

WILL SHASTA ERUPT AGAIN?

The Cascade volcanoes have been growing, exploding, and collapsing for nearly a million years, and the tectonic forces deep within the Earth that created Mt. Shasta are still active. Mt. Shasta is the only Cascade volcano with towns in immediate proximity to its base. McCloud, Dunsmuir, Mount Shasta, and Weed have a collective population of more than ten thousand residents and are all within 15 miles of Shasta's summit. A volcanic explosion, even a moderate one, could destroy the four towns. A 1987 U.S. Geological Survey pamphlet pointedly addressed the eruption hazard to dwellers in the Mt. Shasta area, saying: "An eruption of Mt. Shasta could endanger your life and the lives of your family and friends."

As recently as 1978, and again in the early 1980s, successive minor earthquakes—called "swarm earthquakes"—were detected near Mt. Shasta by geologists and seismologists. Scientists agree that the mountain's history suggests that it erupts roughly once every 250 to 300 years. Therefore, the chance that Shasta will erupt during a person's lifetime is about one in three or four, but there is no reliable way to know when Mt. Shasta will erupt again. The earthquake activity subsided during the late 1980s, but scientists continue to monitor the "sleeping giant."

What does the future hold for Mt. Shasta and the surrounding area? These are questions asked by residents, developers, environmentalists, skiers, spiritualists, Forest Service planners, Native Americans, and legislators. In the end, Mt. Shasta is a plain statement of itself—a bridge between past and present, earth and sky, and we are left to behold and wonder. Whether seen, climbed, contemplated, or immortalized in legend and poetry, Mt. Shasta has secured its place among the great mountains of the world.

·117·

Mt. Shasta's ancient lava flows are a constant reminder of the mountain's fiery origins—and potential to erupt again.

The broad line at the bottom of the photograph is U. S. Highway 97. COURTESY USGS

APPENDIX 1

MUSEUMS, LIBRARIES, & PLACES OF INTEREST

MUSEUMS

MT. SHASTA

The Sisson Museum, located on the grounds of the Mt. Shasta Fish Hatchery, is open year-round. Operated entirely by volunteers, the museum has many permanent displays on historical Siskiyou County—particularly Mt. Shasta—as well as temporary shows that change several times a year. The hatchery itself is the oldest in California.

Location: Hatchery Lane and Old Stage Rd. (off Central I-5 Exit), Mt. Shasta, California
Phone: (916) 926-5508
Hours: Monday-Saturday, 12:00 noon to 4:00 P.M.; Sunday, 1:00 P.M. to 4:00 P.M.
Summer Hours   (beginning Memorial Day): Every day, 10:00 A.M. to 5:00 P.M.

DUNSMUIR

The Dunsmuir Museum has an excellent display of photographs and items representing this historic railroad town, which celebrated its centennial in 1986. Railroad books and other souvenirs are available. The entire downtown business district is on the National Register of Historic Places.

Location: 4101 Pine Street, Dunsmuir, California
Phone: (916) 235-2786
Hours: Monday–Thursday, 11:00 A.M. to 4:00 P.M. Friday–Sunday, 11:00 A.M. to 5:00 P.M.

McCLOUD

The McCloud Heritage Junction Museum includes logging and lumber artifacts from the old days of this early company town. You can also see the old Corliss Steam Engine that ran the mill and provided steam heat to much of McCloud.

Location: 320 Main Street, McCloud, California
Phone: (916) 964-2604
Hours: Tuesday–Saturday, 11:00 A.M. to 3:00 P.M.; Sunday, 1:00 P.M. to 3:00 P.M. (May 1–November 1)

WEED

Weed's museum reflects its lumber-town heritage. Located in the early justice court and police station, it contains old jail cells for visitors to see.

Location: Gilman Avenue, Weed, California
Phone: (916) 938-2352
Hours: Tuesday–Sunday, 11:00 A.M. to 4:00 P.M. (May 1–November 1)

YREKA

The Siskiyou County Museum has displays ranging from prehistoric times to mining, lumbering, railroads, and Native American culture. A two-and-a-half-acre outdoor museum is the scene of special interpretive programs several times during the year. The museum also contains a research library.

Location: 910 South Main Street, Yreka, California
Phone: (916) 842-3836
Hours: Daily, 9:00 A.M. to 5:00 P.M. (summer); Tuesday–Saturday, 9:00 A.M. to 5:00 P.M. (winter) Research library by appointment

KLAMATH FALLS, OREGON

The Klamath County Museum has excellent displays on the area's natural history, early explorers, pioneer settlement, Native American history, and the Modoc wars of the 1870s. It also has an excellent library.

Location: 1451 Main Street, Klamath Falls, Oregon
Phone: (503) 883-4208
Hours: Daily, 9:00 A.M. to 6:00 P.M. (summer);
               daily, 9:00 A.M. to 5:00 P.M. (winter)

LIBRARIES

WEED

The College of the Siskiyous Library in Weed has an excellent special collection of books, manuscripts, photographs, and rare materials all pertaining to the Mt. Shasta volcano.

Location: 800 College Avenue, Weed, California
Phone: (916) 938-5331
Hours: Special collection by appointment

CHICO

The Meriam Library at California State University, Chico has a special Northern California regional history collection of books, manuscripts, photographs, maps, and Edward Stuhl's paintings of the wildflowers of Mt. Shasta.

Location: California State University, Chico, California
Phone: (916) 898-6342
Hours: By appointment

PLACES OF INTEREST

RANGER OFFICES

There are two U.S. Forest Service District Ranger offices in charge of the Mt. Shasta area, one in McCloud and one in Mount Shasta. They have many free maps and information on driving and walking tours to selected points of interst in the area. The local museums also have information and maps to historic places surrounding Mt. Shasta.

Location: Mt. Shasta Ranger District
               204 West Alma Street
               Mt. Shasta, California 96067
Phone: (916) 926-4511
Hours: Daily, 8:00 A.M. to 4:30 P.M.

Location: McCloud Ranger District
               Minnesota Ave. and Hwy 89
               McCloud, CA 96057
Phone: (916) 964-2184
Hours: Daily, 8:00 A.M. to 4:30 P.M.

SKI PARK

Mt. Shasta Ski Park offers summer scenic chairlift rides, guided nature walks, and a special volcanic exhibit. Summer season begins Memorial Day weekend.

Location: 10 miles east of Interstate 5, via Highway 89
Phone: (916) 926-8600

GUIDES

There are several professional guides and outfitters in the Mt. Shasta area who operate under permit from the U.S. Forest Service. You can obtain current listings of these outfitters, as well as brochures and information, from the district ranger offices.

APPENDIX II

SELECTED REFERENCES
ON MT. SHASTA AND THE SURROUNDING AREA

Brewer, William H. *Up and Down California in 1860–64.* Francis Farquhar, ed. 3rd ed. Berkeley: University of California Press, 1974.

Cerve, Wishar S. *Lemuria—The Lost Continent of the Pacific.* San Jose, CA: AMORC, 1931.

Ford, Marilyn, and Edward Stuhl. *Wildflowers of Mt. Shasta.* Klamath Falls, OR: Clementine Publishing Company, 1981.

Harris, Stephen L. *Fire Mountains of the West: The Cascade and Mono Lake Volcanoes.* Missoula, MT: Mountain Press, 1988.

Holsinger, Rosemary. *Shasta Indian Tales.* Happy Camp, CA: Naturegraph Publishers, 1982.

King, Clarence. *Mountaineering in the Sierra Nevada.* New York: James R. Osgood & Co., 1872.

King, Godfre Ray (Guy W. Ballard). *Unveiled Mysteries.* Santa Fe: Saint Germain Press, 1939.

LaLande, Jeff. *First Over the Siskiyous: A Commentary on Peter Skene Ogden's 1826–27 Route of Travel through Northern California and Southwestern Oregon.* Portland, OR: Oregon Historical Society Press, 1987.

Masson, Marcelle. *A Bag of Bones: The Wintu Myths of a Trinity River Indian.* Happy Camp, CA: Naturegraph Publishers, 1966.

Merriam, Dr. C. Hart. *North American Fauna, No. 16, Results of a Biological Survey of Mount Shasta.* Washington, DC: Government Printing Office, 1899.

Miesse, William C. *How Mt. Shasta Got Its Name: A History of the Early Maps of the California-Oregon Border Region.* Mt. Shasta, CA: Montagne Publishing Company. To be published, Fall 1992.

Miesse, William C. *Mt. Shasta—Forgotten Monarch of California: A Legacy in Art, 1841–1941.* Mount Shasta, CA: Montagne Publishing Company. To be published, Fall 1992.

Miller, Joaquin. *Life Amongst the Modocs: Unwritten History.* San Jose, CA: Urion Press, 1982. (text of the first edition published in 1873)

Muir, John. *The Mountains of California.* New York: The Century Company, 1894.

Muir, John. *Steep Trails.* William Frederick Bade, ed. Boston, MA: Houghton Mifflin Co., 1918.

Oliver, Frederick Spencer. *A Dweller on Two Planets.* Los Angeles: Borden Publishing Co., 1940.

Palmquist, Peter E. *Carleton E. Watkins: Photographer of the American West.* Albuquerque, NM: University of New Mexico Press, 1983.

Selter, Andy, and Michael Zanger. The Mt. Shasta Book: *A Guide to Hiking, Climbing, Skiing, and Exploring the Mountain and Surrounding Area.* Berkeley, CA: Wilderness Press, 1989.

Viola, Herman J., and Carolyn Margolis, eds. *Magnificent Voyagers: The U.S. Exploring Expedition of 1838–42.* Washington, DC: Smithsonian Institution Press, 1985.

Wallace, David Rains. *The Klamath Knot.* San Francisco: Sierra Club Books, 1983.